The
STAFF DEVELOPMENT
Handbook

The STAFF DEVELOPMENT Handbook

An Action Guide for Managers and Supervisors

PETER SHEAL

KOGAN PAGE

First published in 1992

Kogan Page Limited
120 Pentonville Road
London N1 9JN

© Peter Sheal, 1992

British Library Cataloguing in Publication Data

A CIP record for this book is available from the British Library.

ISBN 0 7494 04191

Typeset by DP Photosetting, Aylesbury, Bucks
Printed and bound in Great Britain by
Biddles Ltd, Guildford and Kings Lynn

Contents

Acknowledgements

Thank you to Michel Bekhazi, Jon Parsinnen and Ian Leece for reading chapters of this book and giving me their advice and suggestions. Thanks also to Des Robson who produced the Guidelines and Job Tool graphics and gave me additional 'food for thought'.

Extracts from Tom Peters and Nancy Austin's *A Passion for Excellence* (1989) are quoted by kind permission of the publishers, Random House. Material from the US *Training and Development Journal* is used with permission of the American Society for Training and Development. The excerpt from Douglas McGregor's *The Human Side of Enterprise* (1985) is used with permission of the publishers, McGraw-Hill. J. Naisbitt and P. Aburdene's *Megatrends 2000* (1990) is quoted with permission of the publishers, Pan Books.

Introduction

'Effective leadership is full-time people development'. Tom Peters and Nancy Austin, *A Passion for Excellence*.

This book is for managers, supervisors and others who are placed in leadership roles and responsible for the work of other staff. It is intended for managers and supervisors who want to improve their own effectiveness, and the effectiveness of their operations through providing appropriate training and development for their staff.

The book is designed as a handbook to use on-the-job. Each chapter focuses on a specific staff development skill and is self-contained. Additional resources that the manager or supervisor can use will be referenced at the end of the book. The staff training and development process is divided into ten steps, presented in separate chapters. These are:

1. Staff Development – Your Role in Improving Performance

Increasingly the manager's job involves harnessing and developing people's skills to improve the effectiveness and productivity of the operation. This chapter will help you work with your staff in identifying individual objectives and targets for the coming year. These will then be used as a basis for assessing your own and your staff's training and development needs.

Job Tools: Task and Target Sheet and Assessment of Training and Development Effectiveness.

2. How to Introduce New Staff to Your Department

When you arrange for an effective induction programme, you increase a newcomer's chances of success. You help the person adapt to the new work environment and become productive more quickly. This chapter will help you provide an effective induction programme for staff who are new to your operation.

Job Tool: Induction Information Checklist.

3. How to Provide Mentoring and On-the-job Training

Mentoring involves deliberately pairing your skilled and experienced staff with less experienced people so that on-the-job training can be given. This chapter will help you set up a mentoring and on-the-job training system.

Job Tools: Demonstration Preparation Form and Demonstration Checklist.

4. How to Prepare for a Group Training Session

Preparation is the key to successful training. This chapter will help you to prepare an effective group training session. The information and suggestions in this chapter will also help you if you need to prepare a more general presentation or briefing.

Job Tools: Training Preparation Form and Training Feedback Form.

5. How to Conduct a Group Training Session

When you conduct a group training session or presentation the experience can benefit both you and your employees. This chapter will help you to conduct an effective training session. The information and suggestions in the chapter will also help you if you need to make a more general presentation or briefing.

Job Tool: Materials Packing Checklist.

6. How to Improve Performance Through Off-the-job Training

You need to be involved if you want off-the-job training to improve your staff's performance and the productivity of your department. This chapter will help you to select

appropriate off-the-job training courses for your staff, and ensure that what they learn on the course improves their job performance.
Job Tools: Course Selection Checklist and Course Evaluation Form.

7. How to Conduct Effective Team Meetings

Enormous amounts of time and money are wasted in disorganized business meetings. This chapter will help you to assess the effectiveness of the meetings you conduct and attend. It will also suggest some steps for making them more productive in improving staff performance and getting the job done.
Job Tool: Meeting Agenda Form.

8. How to Delegate Work and Responsibilities

Through delegation you can make maximum use of your people's knowledge, skills, and experience. This chapter will help you delegate appropriate tasks and projects to your staff.
Job Tool: Task/Project Delegation Form.

9. How to Coach Your People

Through coaching you can help employees improve their skills and performance. This chapter outlines a systematic approach to coaching sessions and will help you conduct coaching sessions for employees who need to improve their performance.
Job Tool: Coaching Preparation Form.

10. How to Conduct Effective Performance Reviews

Some managers and supervisors feel uncertain about conducting performance reviews, while others don't worry enough about doing a 'good job' in this area. This chapter will help you conduct constructive performance review sessions and work with employees to plan for the future.
Job Tool: Performance Review – Common Errors.

Following Chapter 10 there is a section on aids:

Appendix: How to Develop and Use Training or Presentation Aids

Visual aids can make the difference between your giving a successful or an unsuccessful training session or presentation. Here are some guidelines on how you can develop and use handouts, flipcharts, overhead transparencies and slides. There is also a section on how to select and use video for training sessions or meetings.

Job Tool: Video Assessment Report.

Finally, there is a list of additional references and resources that the manager or supervisor can use.

The book includes staff development tools (forms, checklists etc) for managers and supervisors to use or adapt to their own situation.

Each chapter has the same basic structure consisting of:

- A chapter overview.
- Your current situation – readers are asked to assess their current situation related to this topic area.
- Why this activity is important to the organization.
- The benefits of spending time on this activity.
- Guidelines – how to organize an induction programme, delegate a task, etc.
- Job tools – checklists, diagrams and forms that can be used on the job. With each job tool there is an explanation and suggestions on how the manager or supervisor can use it.
- Common situations.
- Action items.

Terminology

Throughout the book the term 'manager' will be used to refer to anyone responsible for managing or supervising the work of other people. 'Department' will be used to refer to any unit of an organization.

CHAPTER 1

Staff Development – Your Role in Improving Performance

'Today we are replacing the manager as order giver with the manager as teacher, facilitator, and coach. The order giver has all the answers and tells everyone what to do; the facilitator knows how to draw the answers out of those who know them best – the people doing the job'. John Naisbitt and Patricia Aburdene, *Megatrends 2000*.

Managers and supervisors are traditionally the people who give orders. They control the workforce, are responsible for the work and seeing that the employees get it done. In modern organizations however, managers and supervisors need to be increasingly involved in harnessing and developing employees' skills to improve the effectiveness and productivity of the operation.

This chapter will help you to identify departmental objectives and work with your staff in defining individual tasks and targets for the coming year. These tasks and targets will then be used to determine your own and your staff's training and staff development needs.

Your current situation

Using the information at your disposal – business plan, operating plan, requisitions, etc – try to answer the following questions about your department's operations.

1. What improvements in the quality of your product or services do you want to make in the next five years? List some of them.

2. How many professional staff do you have? What are you doing to make sure they are 'up to date'?

3. How many technicians do you have? What are you doing to make sure they are 'up to date'?

4. What new equipment or systems will you be installing in your department over the coming year or two years?

5. How will your people learn how to use the new equipment or systems effectively? What have you planned?

Consider your responses to these questions in the light of the following comments.

Your responses
1. 'Quality' as in 'Quality Assurance' and 'Quality Management' is the buzzword of the 1990s. But if you want to make improvements in your products and services, 'quality' needs to be more than a slogan or buzzword. You need quality people – trained staff who are improving their skills – to do the job.

2 and 3. Your organization recruits professionals and technicians for their specialized knowledge and skills. But they need opportunities to maintain and update their skills if they are going to retain their value to you and the organization. Technicians and professionals also often get 'itchy feet' if they feel they are stagnating and their skills are getting rusty.

4. When you want to install new equipment or systems you plan ahead. In the same way you need to plan training for your people so that the organization and the department gain maximum benefits from new technology.

5. Encouraging people to learn things by trial and error may get the job done in the end. But you can make employees productive

---

more quickly and have fewer mistakes and less 'down-time' if you can arrange training for them.

Why staff training and development are important

There are four main reasons why staff training and development have become more important:

1. Rapid changes in technology and the jobs people do.
2. Immediate and long-term skills shortages.
3. Changes in the expectations and composition of the workforce.
4. Competition and market pressures for improvements in the quality of products and services.

1. Rapid changes in technology and the jobs people do

With accelerating changes in technology and work systems, many traditional industrial and clerical jobs have changed radically or become obsolete. New jobs have been created, particularly in the service and information-based industries. According to the US Labor Department, the average American entering the workforce today will change careers at least three times during his working life. A similar situation applies to European workers, who are now facing the increased labour mobility and skill demands generated by the single market. In order to cope with these changes people need 'portable skills' that will keep them employable when their current jobs change or vanish.

When the organization recruits people they may have the skills and experience to do the job but as the work environment and the job changes, they need to update their skills. If employees don't have opportunities for training, retraining and development, then they and their skills can become 'obsolete'. Similarly, if governments and companies don't provide these opportunities for training and updating, their industries will become obsolete.

2. Immediate and long-term skills shortages

Technological developments have led to a higher percentage of skill and knowledge-based jobs and a greater demand for skilled workers. As a result there is a decreased requirement for unskilled labour.

This is a problem particularly for countries like the UK which have more unskilled than skilled workers. A recent European Community Labour Market Survey showed that only 38 per cent of the UK industrial workforce has received formal skills-based training. This compares with 80 per cent in France, 79 per cent in Italy and 67 per cent in Germany. These figures explain why, even when unemployment has been high in the UK, there have been skills shortages limiting business expansion and the use of new technology and production techniques.

Over the longer term, skills shortages are expected to increase through the greater complexity of jobs and the decreasing numbers of young people entering the workforce. In the West the 'baby boom' generation of the post-World War II period have become the mature employees of the 1970s and 80s. They will reach pensionable age in the early part of the next century when the 'baby bust' of the 1960s and 70s will lead to a reduction in the working population.

Again, the skills gap can only be overcome by an expansion of training, retraining and staff development opportunities. Workers can then move more easily from the unskilled to the skilled labour market, thereby reducing skills shortages and the pool of long-term unemployed and unskilled labour.

3. Changes in the expectations and composition of the workforce

In the past people expected their education and training to last them for a lifetime. Now full-time schooling is recognized as providing only basic foundations for a person's working life. In particular, the increasing proportion of managerial, supervisory and professional workers in the workforce has led to a greater demand for professional development opportunities. This in turn has encouraged a demand from all levels of staff for increased training and development. Nobody wants to become 'obsolete'.

4. Competition and market pressures for improvements in the quality of products and services

There is an increased recognition that only 'quality people' – managers, supervisors and staff with up-to-date knowledge and expertise – can produce high quality products and services. Many organizations are introducing Quality Management and Quality Assurance programmes which require the cooperation, involvement and retraining of the workforce if they are to be successful. Training and staff development are recognized as the primary means for achieving the better quality products and services needed to compete in world markets.

Why your involvement is important

The idea that managers and supervisors should be responsible for training and developing their people is still fairly new but rapidly gaining influence. Your involvement in staff development is important for a number of reasons.

First, leadership means influencing the behaviour of other people positively. One of the best ways of supporting and influencing your people is by helping them to improve their knowledge and skills. To do this you need to encourage continuous learning and improvement on the job. Individual development should become the 'norm' and 'staying the same' a matter for concern.

Second, most problems boil down to 'people problems'. If you list the problems that you face at the moment and analyse them they are often related to poor communication among staff, lack of training, or immature attitudes. By ensuring that your staff are trained and helping them to develop their skills, you can solve many of your 'people problems'. And if you can solve these problems, you are well on the way to success.

Third, many organizations are encouraging their managers and supervisors to become more proactive and less bureaucratic. Decision-making is being pushed 'down the line', with more emphasis being placed on employees taking the initiative, working together in teams and assuming greater responsibility. Staff training and development is one aspect of this proactive approach to management and one way of generating more initiative and flexibility in your people. Certainly, it's more efficient for you to train your staff in how to solve problems and respond to situations themselves, than for you to try to solve all the problems or handle everything yourself.

Fourth, in order to be effective, staff training and development needs to be linked to the job and involve employees' managers and supervisors. No training is 'value free'. If the basic values and philosophy of training are not those of the workplace and conflict with each other, employees feel disappointed and frustrated when they return to the job. Your involvement in training should reduce the possibilities of conflict and frustration. It should also help employees to transfer their newly acquired knowledge and skills to the way they actually do their jobs. Through your involvement in training and development, your knowledge and expertise, not to mention your power as 'the boss', can also be harnessed. You can act as on-the-spot evaluator, trainer and coach. In particular, your authority in performance review and follow-up makes you a powerful agent for change.

Finally, staff development is not a new responsibility but one that you already have. Indeed, you are probably already spending a considerable amount of your time and energy on activities related to staff development. You are involved whenever you:

- discuss future work with your employees;
- introduce a new person to the department;
- get one person to show another how to do something;
- conduct a staff meeting or team discussion;
- delegate work and responsibilities;
- coach one of your people and provide some guidance;
- conduct a performance review meeting.

The issue then is not 'Should I be training and developing my people?' but, 'How can I improve what I'm already doing?'

Despite this necessary involvement, managers and supervisors give many reasons for not wanting to spend time on staff development. Here's a list of the four most common reasons, some of which you may recognize. Below each reason is a response.

1. Look, I'm already overloaded. Just keeping this operation going and dealing with crises is more than enough. I haven't got time to spend on training people. I already have too many jobs to do.

Response: Look again at how you are spending your time. Good management is measured by what your people are doing, not by what you are doing. Your own productivity and the productivity of your operation depend upon your generating more and better quality output from your team. And you have only two ways to raise your people's level of performance – by increasing their capability and by increasing their desire to do the job well. When you train and develop your people you not only increase their ability but their motivation. Obviously developing staff takes time but it improves the effectiveness of your team and the quality of your product or service. It is therefore one of the 'right things' for which you should 'manage' your time.

2. Experience is the best teacher. My boss never helped me or showed me how to do things. I learned how to manage for myself and from my mistakes. So why should I have to worry about training my people?

Response: It usually takes people a long time and many mistakes to learn from experience. Not only that, but experience doesn't always teach us the best way to do things. When we learn the basics wrongly, it can prove very difficult to unlearn the 'lessons of experience'. Also, some people don't learn from their mistakes and gain confidence from their 'experience' to continue in the 'old way'. In the end, one year of poor performance repeated 35 times may provide someone with a gold watch but doesn't contribute much to the organization's bottom line.

Finally, you *should* 'worry' about training your people because in this way you can reduce the time it takes for them to be effective and 'safe' on the job. You wouldn't ask someone to learn to drive 'by experience'. They take lessons first so that they get the basics right and survive to take the driving test.

3. I employed my people as trained staff. This is not a place for people to learn – they should have done that before. They are here to produce.

Response: They may have learned enough before to handle their current jobs but if your organization is progressing, their jobs will change. They will produce more and to a higher standard if there are periodic opportunities for them to develop and improve their skills. If your people feel they are in 'dead-end' jobs with no opportunity to learn and improve, they won't produce very much and will leave as soon as they get the chance.

4. Training and staff development are personnel or training department responsibilities. It's nothing to do with me.
Response: You know much more about the jobs in your department and your people's needs than the personnel or training department. Your staff won't be able to do their jobs well unless they've been trained well, and they won't be trained unless you make arrangements to get it done.

Benefits of staff development

What's in it for the organization
Your involvement in staff development can help the organization by improving the following.

● Staff recruitment and retention. The prospect of on-the-job training and development tends to attract good quality job applicants. Staff turnover can also be reduced because trained people who have opportunities for development gain more job satisfaction and enjoy the sense that their potential is recognized.

● Use of new technology and work systems. In the largest companies there is often lots of technology but little 'in use' and people feel left behind. The technology – including computer equipment, manufacturing systems, communications – is changing so rapidly that training departments aren't able to keep up with the amount and variety of training that's required. As the 'boss' you are in the best position to arrange on-the-job training for individuals or small groups that are not big enough to form a class.

● Quality of products and services. Quality improvements lead to greater customer satisfaction with your department's work and with the organization as a whole.

● Identification of future supervisory and management personnel. Through your involvement in staff development you can help to identify people with management and supervisory potential and thereby promote the long-term future of the organization.

What's in it for you
Your involvement in staff development can lead to improvements in the following.

● What you are already doing. By paying attention to staff development you can ensure that you and your people are learning from problems and experiences rather than repeating them. For example, you may spend a lot of time correcting mistakes that your employees make. If you use your time instead to coach your people and show them what is needed, you can develop their skills, give them more responsibility and save your own time in the future.

● The future capability of you and your staff. Unlike equipment, people should increase in value over time as they gain knowledge, expertise and experience. If you and your staff constantly update your knowledge and skills you won't get left behind and will be able to cope better with changes in workload and job requirements.

● Your own performance and promotion prospects. You need to avoid the classic mistake of trying do everything yourself. If you can improve your people's skills and train them to take on more responsibility, you will be better equipped to take on greater responsibilities yourself.

What's in it for your people
Your involvement in staff development can lead to the following improvements for your people.

IDENTIFYING TASKS, TARGETS AND NEEDS

1. IDENTIFY DEPARTMENTAL GOALS AND OBJECTIVES ☐

2. IDENTIFY DEPARTMENTAL TRAINING AND
   DEVELOPMENT NEEDS ☐

3. IDENTIFY YOUR OWN TASKS, TARGETS AND NEEDS ☐

4. IDENTIFY EMPLOYEE TASKS, TARGETS AND NEEDS ☐

5. MEET INDIVIDUALS TO DISCUSS TASKS, TARGETS
   AND NEEDS ☐

6. AGREE ON TRAINING AND DEVELOPMENT NEEDED ☐

7. PLAN FOR TRAINING AND DEVELOPMENT ☐

Figure 1.1

● Job security. Employees who become more versatile and multi-skilled obviously have greater job security as they can adjust to changes in the nature of their work.

● Job potential. Staff who are developing their skills and want to improve themselves can take on increasing responsibilities. They have greater opportunities for promotion or for favourable transfers.

- Motivation and job satisfaction. When employees participate in staff development activities they feel that management is paying attention to them and this often increases their motivation and satisfaction with the job.

Staff training and development is tied up with achieving your operational goals and you should plan for it just as you plan your budget, staffing and materials requirements.

The guidelines in Figure 1.1 outline a systematic approach to establishing operational goals, tasks and targets for your staff. This approach will also help you to identify your staff's training and development needs.

Guidelines for identifying tasks, targets and needs

The guidelines are shown in the form of a checklist to make them easy to use. The notes below describe each of the steps in turn and provide further information and suggestions.

1. Identify departmental goals and objectives.
Business plans and operating plans define an organization's goals and objectives. These can be divided into those which deal with new directions and workload and those which relate to improving or maintaining current operations and activities.

Your business plan defines where your organization should be in five years' time. Look at this plan to identify the departmental goals and objectives relating to new directions and workload. You may need to acquire new markets, develop new products and services, operate new technology, increase productivity, or improve your quality targets. Ask yourself questions like:

- What are we going to do over the next year towards these objectives?
- How are we going to do it?

We tend to think of the budget we will need, the equipment or materials we should order to accomplish these objectives. But goals and objectives are achieved or not achieved through people.

You need to look at whether your staff are already equipped or whether they will need additional knowledge and skills to achieve these objectives.

2. Identify departmental training and development needs.
Sometimes because of a takeover, merger or other fundamental changes an organization needs to change so much that shifts in the 'organizational culture' are required. For example, companies which have been privatized and now have to compete in the private sector have had to change their organizational 'values'. Management and employees have needed to develop more competitive and 'service-oriented' attitudes. Similarly, national airlines losing their 'protected status' and subsidies have needed to become more competitive and improve their customer service. These fundamental changes and shifts in emphasis often require everyone to participate in new training programmes so that they understand the new requirements and can operate effectively in a fresh environment.

Even when the changes are not 'revolutionary', new goals and objectives generate additional training and development needs. To identify these, ask yourself questions like:

- What marketing and sales training do staff need to win the new markets?
- What skills training do staff need to produce new products and services or improve our current products and services?
- How can we best train people to use the new equipment and work systems effectively?
- How can we improve our sales training and customer service so that we gain more new orders and repeat business?
- Will we need to work more closely with other departments? What do staff need to know about these departments and the broader organization?

As well as the new goals and objectives, there are also the department's 'maintenance' requirements. Here you need to identify what is needed to maintain current operations and a healthy department. Some questions to consider are:

- Do we have any new recruits or people transferred into our department who need to go through an induction programme?
- How many people are resigning and why? How can we reduce our loss of skilled people?
- What on-the-job training will the new people need, how will it be done and who will do it?
- Do we need to prepare someone for promotion? Who? How can we best prepare him or her to be foreman or supervisor?
- Who will take the promoted person's job? What does he or she need to know and be able to do?
- What needs are there for continuing professional or technical development?
- Do we need to prepare some people for redundancy or retirement? Who? How can we best prepare them?
- What's our safety record like? How can we improve it? Who needs first aid or safety training?

3. Identify your own individual tasks, targets and needs.
Considering your departmental goals and objectives, you need to identify which new goals and objectives are the highest priority. These are usually the ones which you need to be most closely involved with or work on personally. The new goals and objectives will be most critical and receive most attention from top management. Problems and mistakes there will attract most attention; conversely, success in new 'business' will be recognized and benefit the reputation of the department and yourself. Those tasks which have become 'maintenance tasks' should be delegated so that you can concentrate on the new work. Use the Task and Target Sheet, Figure 1.2, to list your own tasks and targets for the coming year and the necessary completion dates. Then consider what training and development you require to work on these projects. You might need to learn a new computer program, attend a local or national conference, and learn more about the work of another department. When you think of staff training and development, don't overlook your own needs.

TASK AND TARGET SHEET

NAME:_____

JOB TITLE:_____

TASKS/TARGETS FOR NEXT YEAR:

1._____
                    Completion Date:_____

2._____
                    Completion Date:_____

3._____
                    Completion Date:_____

4._____
                    Completion Date:_____

5._____
                    Completion Date:_____

6._____
                    Completion Date:_____

7._____
                    Completion Date:_____

TRAINING/DEVELOPMENT REQUIRED:

_____
_____
_____
_____
_____

Figure 1.2

4. Identify employee tasks, targets and needs.
Now that you have decided what you will work on and your degree of involvement, look at your members of staff. List the new jobs and consider each person and his or her current workload. Some questions to consider here are:

- Who has done this kind of job before? Who is already doing this kind of job? That person might take the leading role in the new task or project.
- Who needs to learn how to do this? That person might assist you or the first person and be prepared to take over at a later stage.
- What does the employee need to know or be able to do in order to accomplish this task? Answers to this question will help you to identify the person's training and development needs.

As you answer these questions, consider also the individual needs that have arisen from performance review sessions, individual coaching or your discussions with employees about their career plans and personal development. What training or development do they need to improve their skills and become more valuable to the department?

For each member of your staff use the Task and Target Sheet, Figure 1.2, to identify their tasks and targets for the coming year. Then note some training and development activities which may help them achieve these tasks and targets. When you meet employees, use your completed sheets as a basis for discussion.

5. Meet individuals to discuss tasks, targets and needs.
Meet with each individual employee before you finally decide upon his or her tasks and targets for the coming year. This discussion may be part of the performance review meeting when you plan for the future. However, if you discuss previous performance and then continue with a detailed discussion of next year's work, you may 'overload' the performance review meeting. Usually it is better to have two meetings – one at the beginning of the performance period which discusses in detail future tasks and targets, then one at the end of the performance

period which looks back on the year's performance and sets the stage for the future. This performance review meeting is described in Chapter 10, How to Conduct Effective Performance Reviews.

At the goal-setting meeting you should work together with the employee to identify individual tasks and targets for the coming year and agree upon action. During the discussion, use questions to obtain the employee's own ideas and suggestions. You might use questions like:

- What kind of tasks do *you* think you are best equipped to do?
- What would you like to do in the coming year?
- What changes might be made to this task to make it easier, more interesting or more productive?
- If there isn't a fixed deadline, ask 'When do you think this can realistically be done?'
- If there is a fixed deadline say, 'This is the deadline. How can we meet it? What will you need in order to complete this job on schedule?'

When you involve employees in this kind of discussion, you generate greater commitment and accountability. By participating in establishing their own tasks and targets, employees also tend to set higher and more challenging goals. This is because people tend to expect more of themselves than you expect of them. Research also shows that this kind of goal-setting, rather than criticism, is most effective in improving performance. Specific challenging goals, including realistic deadlines, will motivate your people and lead to better performance than easy or vague goals such as 'do your best'. The goals you agree upon, however, should be feasible because unrealistic tasks and targets lead to employees becoming demoralized.

People also learn more when they are involved in discussions about their future and can identify their own needs. As a result of your discussion, be prepared to change some things to gain the employee's commitment and enthusiasm. For further information on this see Chapter 8, How to Delegate Work and Responsibilities.

6. Agree on training and development needed
If the employee needs to participate in some training or development activities, discuss the possible options. These might include one or a combination of the following:

- On-the-job training conducted by an experienced employee.
- Attendance at off-the-job training courses.
- Open or distance learning using books, TV, computers, learning centres, etc.
- Delegation and responsibility for a task.
- Coaching from yourself or your representative.

Again, discuss which methods might be most effective in helping the employee get the job done. If the employee requires computer skills, it may be difficult for him or her to get into a formal training course fairly soon. On-the-job training may be more effective and the employee may have some ideas about who might give that training. Listen to the employee's preferences and ensure commitment to the task by involving him or her as much as possible in the decision-making.

7. Plan for training and development
Based upon your discussions with each employee, plan some training and development activities for the forthcoming year.

Common situations

When you do something new or change things, difficulties can arise. Here are some situations you might need to deal with when you become involved in staff development. Below each situation is a suggested response.

Situation: You are interested in improving your own and your people's skills but need to get your boss's support.
Response: Performance review time provides an opportunity to discuss the improvements you want to make in your own performance and the performance of your people. Let your boss

know you are going to spend time on staff development and about the benefits this will bring to the organization.

Situation: You've left people alone for years and suddenly you want to train and develop them. Some of your people are puzzled or sceptical of your 'new approach'.
Response: At the regular staff meeting point out that you are trying to improve your own skills and that you want people to look at ways of improving their own performance. Most people are likely to be enthusiastic at the idea. Some longer-term employees may need reassurance that this isn't a threat to them. Meet with each of them privately and let them suggest some areas for development or discuss ways to achieve 'their aims'. For someone who has been in the organization a long time, off-the-job training courses may well prove more stimulating and useful than on-the-job training.

Situation: You have some senior people who plateaued years ago and are cruising along happily towards retirement.
Response: Meet with them to discuss their current workload and what they might do in future to develop their skills and take on increasing responsibility. Again, off-the-job training courses may well prove more stimulating than internal training. The off-the-job course, however, may well be followed by some on-the-job practice and new responsibilities. Look at the chapters on 'Mentoring and On-the-job Training', 'How to Improve Performance through Off-the-job Training', and 'Delegating Work and Responsibilities' for more ideas.

Action items

Leadership involves improving *your own* performance as well as working with your people to improve *their* performance. Use the checklist, Figure 1.3, to assess your effectiveness in training and developing your employees and to highlight those parts of this handbook which will be particularly useful to you.

As you make decisions on whether you are OK or need to work on a particular skill, make some additional comments or suggest ideas for improvement in the column provided. If you are not involved in a particular activity, for example orientation, you might consider whether you need to get involved.

When you have completed the checklist, consider the results carefully and, if possible, discuss them with a colleague in order to identify and clarify some high-priority needs.

SELF-ASSESSMENT:
TRAINING AND DEVELOPMENT EFFECTIVENESS

SKILL	OK	NEEDS WORK	COMMENT/ IMPROVEMENT
1. Identifying when a person needs training			
2. Introducing a new person to the work of your department			
3. Arranging for one person to mentor another			
4. Preparing training sessions			
5. Conducting training sessions			
6. Selecting and following - up on off-the-job training courses			
7. Conducting team meetings and discussions			
8. Delegating work and responsibilities			
9. Coaching your people			
10. Conducting performance reviews			

Figure 1.3

CHAPTER 2

How to Introduce New Staff to Your Department

Alice tried another question. "What sort of people live about here?"

"In that direction", the Cat said, waving its right paw around, "lives a Hatter; and in that direction", waving the other paw, "lives a March Hare. Visit either you like: they're both mad".

"But I don't want to go among mad people", Alice remarked.

"Oh, you can't help that", said the Cat, "we're all mad here. I'm mad. You're mad".

"How do you know I'm mad ?", said Alice.

"You must be", said the Cat, "Or you wouldn't have come here".

Lewis Carroll, *Alice in Wonderland*.

Generally, we're not 'all mad here' even though a newcomer to the organization might sometimes be forgiven for thinking so. The Mad Hatter and the March Hare may not be on your staff list but the newcomer, like Alice, often feels confused and rather disoriented. As the manager or supervisor, one of your key tasks is to reduce this confusion – to introduce new staff to the organization, the job, the people they will work with and to you as the boss. You need to increase newcomers' chances of success and to integrate them into the work group.

Effective induction, or orientation as it's known in the USA, ideally consists of two stages: a company programme usually conducted by the personnel or training department, and a department or unit programme. This chapter focuses on the second stage of induction – the department or unit programme. This is the stage you are responsible for and which establishes the relationship between new people and the people they work with (including yourself), and the organization. The purpose of this chapter is to help you develop an effective induction programme for staff who are new to your operation.

Your current situation

Think back to the first day with your current employer. What were your feelings, your impressions of the new job and your supervisor. What happened on that first day? List three or four experiences.

How might any negative experiences have been avoided through good induction?

Who has required induction to your department in the past year? Include not only new staff, but people who have been transferred to your department and visiting managers.

Have you and your department got an induction plan or package for new people? If so, what does it consist of?

Why induction is important

When people look back on their first day in a new job there are generally more negative experiences than positive ones. Comments like the following are common:

I was confused and the supervisor wasn't there.
I was just given manuals to read for the first week. I felt forgotten.
When I arrived I found they'd decided to move me to another job in another unit.
I met two people who were leaving and they told me all about the organization – all the problems they'd had and the way management behaved.

The supervisor was threatening. He told me that if I didn't do well, I'd be transferred.

Organizations spend large amounts of time and money in installing new equipment and processes. This systematic effort is often in sharp contrast to the haphazard manner in which many new staff are 'installed' in their new jobs. Poor or ineffective induction can have a number of consequences. First: high rates of staff turnover and increased recruitment costs. When you lose personnel you lose money. For example, in the USA it costs $6000 per person to recruit someone, yet as many as 50 to 60 per cent of new employees leave their jobs within the first seven months. (American estimates are that replacement costs for a first level supervisor are $60,000 and for a second level manager $50,000.) In the UK approximately 20 per cent of new employees leave within the first three months of starting a job. These figures are bad enough, but the situation is self-perpetuating. Early leavers damage the organization's reputation as an employer, and this often makes it even more difficult to find and keep good quality recruits.

It takes a long time and a great deal of effort to recruit people and develop them to the level of performance you want. When companies have invested in systematic induction programmes however, there have been significant reductions in staff turnover.

A second consequence of poor induction is low quality work from new people, high error rates, and unnecessarily lengthy training periods. An effective induction programme can establish quality standards at the beginning of a new person's time with you, prevent errors, and provide a foundation for any future training.

A third consequence is the establishment of unproductive working practices. If the induction period is not successful and the new person becomes long-term 'deadwood', the cost to the company is high. Thus the hours invested in providing an effective induction may save hundreds of hours of corrective coaching in the months and years to come.

Studies in a variety of organizations, ranging from Apple Computer and Texas Instruments to the US Department of

Education, have shown that care and attention to induction can ensure the same high levels of productivity and efficiency among new people as planned installation and preventive maintenance achieves from new equipment. Moreover, unlike machinery which begins to deteriorate from the day it operates, trained and motivated staff can make an increasingly effective contribution as years go by.

The objectives of an effective induction programme are to assist newcomers to adapt rapidly to their new work environment and to help them become effective in their jobs as quickly as possible. Induction ideally consists of two stages:

- Induction to the organization or company.
- Induction to the department or unit.

The induction to the organization is usually designed and conducted by the personnel or training department. Obviously, you should know what this induction consists of, and it would be very useful for you to attend so that you can link the organizational overview with your own induction programme. You may also learn something new!

Department or unit induction, however, is the stage you are mainly responsible for and establishes the relationships between new people and their colleagues, yourself and the organization. You need to treat this induction as the first step in the new person's career with the organization rather than a separate one-off activity. The induction that you provide sets the pattern for a person's longer-term motivation, commitment and contribution to your department.

You need to provide induction not only for people who are new to your organization, but for staff who are joining your department from other departments on a temporary or permanent basis. These 'transfers' need to know many of the things that new staff need to know and in particular the differences between their previous department and yours. Your orientation programme should be modified and adapted to their needs. In the same way, elements of your induction programme may prove useful for orienting managers or supervisors who are visiting, or on temporary assignment, to your department.

Reasons for poor induction

Many reasons are given for ineffective or missing induction programmes. Here's a list of the most common and following each reason is a response.

1. We don't spend much time on induction around here. We're too busy. I learned the job without all this spoon-feeding.
Response: By giving an effective induction, you can save time. The new person can learn more quickly, and less of your time needs to be spent in giving additional instructions or in dealing with mistakes the new employee has made. As for your learning the job without induction, some people may swim when they're thrown in at the 'deep end' but others can drown . 'Sink or swim' isn't a very efficient or humane way to treat people.

2. I haven't got time.
Response: As the effectiveness of induction has a significant impact on early resignations, absenteeism and future staff productivity, you need to *make time* to organize and participate in induction programmes. Induction should be a Priority 1 task. New people constantly ask themselves questions: 'Will I like this job?', 'Can I work for this supervisor?', 'Am I going to fit in here?' They need to believe that they are welcome and recognized. If you haven't got time to spend with them, you are sending the message that they and their jobs are not very important.

3. Somebody else should do it.
Response: Often managers or supervisors expect the company to provide induction, and the company expects them to do it. Ultimately, however, the responsibility for induction rests with you. Through a combination of department induction, company induction, and on-the-job training you should arrange for new people to have an effective induction and one that responds to their needs.

4. Perhaps I won't be able to answer all the new employee's questions.
Response: Don't attempt to be the source of all information and the fount of all wisdom for the new employee. If you don't know the answer to a specific question, you can probably put the new person in touch with someone in the organization or in your department who does have the answer. In particular, don't attempt to conduct the orientation alone. Use one of your senior staff as a mentor and others as resource people.

5. He's done this kind of job before. He shouldn't need induction.
Responses: With employees now expected to change jobs several times in their careers and women returning to work as their children grow up, new employees are often experienced in the job. This does not mean however that they don't need induction. Like other new employees, they need an induction to the organization and to feel they are noticed and accepted by the work group.

6. I don't really need her now.
Response: The reasons why you needed the new person may well have become less urgent by the time that new person arrives. Similarly, the new person may not be very productive at first – she can't answer your pressing problems. For these reasons there may be a tendency for you to ignore her and neglect her induction. Don't.

7. We'll give him some information checklists to use and manuals to read.
Response: Supervisors who want to provide a systematic induction sometimes give new people a lot of paperwork, manuals and information checklists to read. This is frequently at the cost of reducing the vital 'people contact' part of the induction. Especially in the early stages of induction, you should focus on getting new people 'settled in' rather than cramming their heads with detailed information.

8. We've hired her to do a job – not to develop her.
Reponse: You may have hired someone to do a specific job but she may be capable of doing a better job or more jobs than you

imagine. If you take a restricted view of the person, you may not make full use of her capabilities and both you and the organization will lose out.

9. *I believe in on-the-job training. He can find out things from the others. For a start he can sit next to Ann who's been doing the job for years.*
Response: On-the-job training sounds fine but too often it means no training at all with the new person left to pick up things as he or she goes along. Sitting next to Ann may also be a good idea, but both the new person and Ann need to know what's to be learned and the learning should be organized and systematic (see Chapter 4, Mentoring and On-the-job Training).

Benefits of effective induction

What's in it for you
By providing an effective induction programme you achieve the following.

● You ensure that new people become independent sooner on routine operations so that you and other members of staff don't have to spend so much time on formal guidance. Through becoming productive more quickly, new people can make a better contribution to the work of the department.

● You demonstrate how much you value new people, and show your willingness to give time and attention to them and the other people who work for you.

● You give a message to new people and impress your own boss with the systematic way in which the department is organized.

● You prevent others, particularly those who are discontented, doing the job instead. You don't want to find that your new people have been introduced to work avoidance and developed a negative attitude towards you, the department and the organization as a whole.

- Finally, you will feel 'good' when you see how relaxed and relieved the new employee feels as a result of your induction programme.

What's in it for new people
Through an effective induction, new staff gain the following.

- Motivation from early acceptance and recognition from their boss and colleagues. They are integrated into the work group more quickly.

- A reduction in anxiety because new people know that they are gaining information and an understanding of the organization's rules and regulations in a systematic way.

- A feeling of security from early knowledge of the methods and expectations of the department.

- Greater self-respect. New people feel that their manager and the organization have respect for them as potentially valuable individuals, rather than as numbers on a manpower report or names to fill job slots.

Once the message that 'You belong', 'You can contribute', is understood, then the adaptation and learning processes can be substantially shortened. New people will have the desire and confidence to learn and to work productively.

Induction guidelines

The basic guidelines for organizing an induction programme are shown in Figure 2.1. These guidelines are shown in the form of a checklist to make them easy to use. The notes below describe each of the steps in turn and provide further information and suggestions on how to follow the guidelines.

Preparation
During the first few weeks and months of a new job there's a lot

INDUCTION GUIDELINES

PREPARATION
1. ASSIGN SOMEONE AS MENTOR ☐
2. MEET WITH MENTOR AND PLAN INDUCTION ☐
3. PREPARE INDUCTION SCHEDULE AND
                      INFORMATION PACKAGE ☐
4. INFORM OTHER STAFF ☐
5. PREPARE WORK AREA ☐
6. PREPARE FOR FIRST MEETING ☐

MEETINGS AND FOLLOW-UP
USING INDUCTION INFORMATION CHECKLIST

1st DAY: GETTING TO KNOW YOU ☐

1st WEEK: LEARNING ABOUT THE JOB AND THE TEAM ☐

1st MONTH: LEARNING ABOUT THE JOB
                      AND THE ORGANIZATION ☐

FOLLOW-UP

Figure 2.1

for new people to learn about the department's operations and its people. You should ask yourself, 'What does this person need to know and be able to do in order to get through the first day/first week/and first months?' The 'need to know' information and skills will take up the bulk of your orientation. Don't limit yourself too narrowly though. Induction should provide as complete a picture as possible to help the new employee understand why he or she is there – what role their job plays in the overall organization.

By planning this learning process systematically, you can ensure the early effectiveness of new people. As preparation steps, you should carry out the following.

1. Assign someone as mentor

The mentor's role is to act as a helpful workmate, give friendly guidance and generally ease the new person into the work environment. In particular, the mentor can answer questions which the new person might feel stupid asking the boss. Mentors can also introduce new people to the informal networks of the workplace and provide an initial social contact. If possible, the mentor you select should:

- be of a similar age, and have a similar job to the new person;
- have fairly short service so that he or she remembers all the little points that were a source of anxiety when *he or she* started work;
- be sympathetic to the needs of new people. Some experienced staff enjoy the advantage that their superior knowledge gives them and withhold important information about the job;
- have a positive attitude towards the work and the department.

The mentor will be acting as your and the department's representative and should know that.

2. Meet with the mentor and plan induction

Brief the mentor on his or her role. You and the mentor should think of things that the new person can do so that he or she gets an opportunity to learn more about the operation, works with others and makes a positive contribution to the work of your department.

3. Prepare an induction schedule and information package

Work with the mentor to prepare a schedule for the first day and a tentative schedule for the first week. This will ensure that you, the new person, and other members of staff who will be involved, know what's happening. The schedule for the first day might be like an agenda with the time, activity and person responsible given. Don't overfill the schedule though: provide some free time for the new person to spend in his or her work area to assimilate information, read documentation or just get to know people.

A brief handbook or information package on your department can also be a useful guide for new people. You might develop one of your experienced staff by getting him or her to produce the material. Alternatively, you might choose the mentor to do the job or someone who is still new enough to remember what newcomers most need to know when they start.

4. Inform other staff

Involve other staff besides the mentor in getting ready for the newcomer and helping him/her adjust to the new environment. Rather than let the grapevine do its worst, inform the rest of your staff about the new person and their role in the group. Provide those people who are involved with a copy of the induction schedule. You also need to inform the person who the newcomer will meet first – the receptionist or secretary – so that the new person is well received. You might also arrange a 'welcome coffee'. It's usual to have a farewell 'get together' when someone leaves so why not arrange for something when a new person joins the department?

5. Prepare the work area

Make sure you also prepare the work area. Before the new person arrives, ensure that supplies, materials and equipment which are required immediately are in the work area. This should make the new person feel welcome and encourage him or her to be productive early on.

6. Prepare for the first meeting
Review the person's application form or employee file and decide what you need to find out that isn't in the paperwork or what points you need additional information on. The areas covered in the initial discussion might include the new person's:

- work experience – what he or she did in previous jobs;
- previous education and training, particularly those aspects which relate to the current job;
- interests. For example, computer interests may indicate that the newcomer might be used for computer work or as a mentor for computer training.

As part of your final preparation for this meeting, contact the new person. Make sure that he or she has a clear reporting time and place. When you contact the new person beforehand you show your interest and this will reduce nervousness.

Meetings and follow-up

1. The first day: getting to know you
When people communicate with each other two levels of communication are involved: the *information level* and the *relationship level*. The information level includes facts and opinions, whereas the relationship level involves feelings and the relationships between people. Particularly when people have only just met and in highly charged situations – like the first day in a new job – the relationship level is primary. It's essential therefore that you meet the new person on the first day and establish a relationship. Don't keep the newcomer waiting or treat him or her as if they are the last thing on your list of priorities.

The most important tasks at this first meeting are for you and the new person to learn about each other and to establish a good working relationship. As mentioned previously, you might discuss the new person's work experience, previous education and training and interests. Through this discussion you should try to develop the relationship, rather than seem to be interrogating the newcomer for additional information. Express genuine interest and listen to the person. In particular, you need to identify any anxieties or concerns that have arisen because of the new job and help the new person to resolve them. Induction isn't a one-way process where only the new person is learning. You are also learning – not only about the newcomer and their experience, but how their skills and experience can best be used in your operation.

This first meeting can provide an opportunity for you to explain the department's 'mission' and how it fits into the 'big picture'. You might give general information on the department's objectives and about the way work is done. For example, how much freedom of movement there is, the degree of initiative expected and the amount of autonomy people have. It's common for some managers to sit down with the new person on the first morning and review the requirements of the job by looking at the job description and discussing the responsibilities in detail. However, an in-depth discussion of the job on the first day is often premature – the new person won't retain many of the details. Content yourself with an informal and general overview of the job and its responsibilities.

On this first day then, you need to make the newcomer feel relaxed and help him or her deal with immediate practical matters – your mentor can take the person on a tour of the unit/department, introduce him or her to the people they will work most closely with and help the newcomer settle into the job.

Suggested documentation: a first day's package of information might include:

- Organization chart/structure of the organization showing how your department fits in. You might explain how the new person fits into the department.
- Induction schedule for the first day and first week. Identify the contact people for each activity on the schedule.
- Staff listing. It's easy to forget names when you're introduced to a lot of people on the first day.
- Location maps, diagrams of the work area and perhaps the community area.

Discuss this information with the new person and clarify or

expand on it where necessary. Additional pages can be added to the package as the new person goes through the induction period – but you should avoid overburdening the newcomer with too many documents or checklists on the first day.

At a *review meeting* at the end of the first day you might:

– discuss what the newcomer has done and learnt during the day. Let the person use the Induction Information Checklist to identify areas where he or she wants more information;
– elicit questions about the department's operations. New people often think that to ask a lot of questions, particularly of the boss, will make them appear stupid or incompetent. It's always better to encourage new people to ask questions and get answers, rather than leave them in uncertainty;
– discuss the week's induction schedule. This schedule should be rather less detailed than the first day's programme with just the major activities indicated. Discuss the schedule with the mentor beforehand and with the new person at the end of the first day. The schedule can then be adjusted according to the new person's needs.

2. The first week: learning about the job and the team

It usually takes a week before details of the new job have any meaning. During that week you should work with the mentor to ensure that the newcomer is kept fairly busy. If the person has little to do, he or she may feel embarrassingly isolated and out of place. You need to check on progress but not too frequently or the newcomer may feel you're breathing down his or her neck.

Suggested documentation: additional pages for the induction package might include:

• Written information on the work/projects of the department and who is responsible for handling them. The new person can refer to the information, read it on his/her own and discuss it with you at the end of the week.
• The new person's job description – this can be used as a general guide and as an aid to any discussion or job instruction that is required.

At the end of the first week you should conduct a *review meeting* with the new person. At this meeting you might do the following.

- discuss what the newcomer has done and learned during the week;
- elicit questions about the department's operations;
- discuss the job description and specific responsibilities. Look for areas where the new person may be strong and which can be developed further, and areas where he may need some assistance and training. You should treat any need for training in a constructive way so as to overcome any insecurity or defensiveness in the new person;
- explain the probationary period and procedures. The probationary period should be a positive constructive period in which the new person gets a chance to demonstrate his/her skills and to learn new ones. Don't present the probationary period as a threat;
- discuss the remainder of the month's induction schedule. This should just indicate the major activities. Again, the schedule should have been discussed with the mentor beforehand and adjusted according to the new person's needs. You and the mentor should have asked yourselves, 'What should this new person know/be able to do by the end of the first month?' Any assistance or training required in order to deal with specific job responsibilities should be scheduled. Let the new person use the Induction Information Checklist to identify areas where he or she wants more information.

3. The first month: learning about the job and the organization
Studies show that it takes at least three weeks for a newcomer to become familiar with his new environment and begin to form bonds of cooperation. People need to find out who can help them solve certain problems and what informal methods are available to get assistance. By the end of the first month the new person should know the people in the department and be establishing contacts with other people in the organization. He or she should know who does what, and who to contact for what.

You can enhance the success of the induction by following-up on the new person's progress and providing assistance with any problems which may arise. Informal follow-up involves your day-to-day interest in the newcomer's progress and the conversations that arise as you walk around your department. Such follow-up conversations usually involve the following.

- Personal recognition through the use of the person's first name.
- Reference to previous meetings and discussions. This shows that you remember things of concern to the new person and again demonstrates individual recognition.
- A positive check on a specific aspect of the job. Don't just ask general questions like 'How are things going?' These can be answered by a simple 'Alright thanks'. Instead, ask a genuine question about what the new person is working on. You may even ask him or her to show you the particular task he/she is working on. Make sure that in these critical first weeks new people are doing work they can handle. If you don't, you may be storing up future problems.
- Watch for any uncertainty, hesitation or signs that the new person may need help and encourage any requests for assistance. New people need to know who they can go to with problems, and you should make sure that these people – mentors, supervisors or foremen – know that it's their responsibility to help newcomers succeed.

Suggested documentation:

- Listings of regular contacts outside the unit or department.
- Performance appraisal information and forms.

In the *review meeting* at the end of the first month you might:

- discuss with the newcomer what he/she has done and learned during the month;
- elicit questions about the department's operations;
- discuss the job description and responsibilities in more detail

and consider the need for any further induction assistance or on-the-job training;

- discuss progress through the probationary period. Make it clear to the new person that you and the mentor are focusing on making him or her a success. Don't make the person feel that you keep checking to find fault.
- explain and discuss the organization's performance appraisal procedures. The new person should know what's expected of him or her. When you provide information on the appraisal criteria the newcomer can keep in mind what he or she will be evaluated upon and develop positive habits during this formative period.

Follow-up

During the probationary period, you need to follow-up on the new person's progress. Through contact with the mentor and directly with the new person him or her self you can provide appropriate guidance and support. In this way you can ensure the new person's integration into the work group and that he or she becomes a regular member of the team.

The induction information checklist

You might use the checklist, Figure 2.2, during the first month of induction. You and the mentor can review the checklist and –

- Decide what items you need to add/delete to tailor the checklist to your circumstances.
- Decide which items need to be covered on the first day and during the first weeks/months. No one should be expected to absorb all this information in one day.

Common situations

Situation: There isn't enough time for induction because of the pressure of work and the need to make the new person productive.

Response: The induction of new staff should be a first priority for you and your organization. Impressions gained by new people during induction can influence their view of the organization for many years. The new person will settle in, be effective and productive more quickly if he or she receives a good induction.

Situation: The new person needs to read the policy and procedures manuals to learn about the department's work and the job.
Response: Ask the mentor or another employee to review these manuals to decide which parts are most important for the new employee. Direct the new person to read only those parts at first.

Situation: Do part-timers need induction?
Response: There's a tendency to ignore part-timers and regard them as temporary staff. This often proves a self-fulfilling prophecy. If you don't expect people to stay long, that communicates itself to them and they *won't* stay. By providing an induction and making new people feel 'part of the family', you increase the likelihood that they *will* stay.

Situation: What about older people returning to work after some time away. What do they need?
Response: People returning to work often need to be trained to use new equipment like computers. The person doing the training needs to avoid terminology and should be less concerned with impressing the returning person than with helping him or her.

Older people may also not be used to group training and may feel out of place in 'a roomful of kids'. They generally need and prefer one-to-one assistance with a sympathetic mentor, perhaps someone around the same age.

Situation: At the end of the first week, the new person comes to you and asks for a transfer. He or she feels that this job isn't for them.
Response: It's likely that the new person will be upset and may be reacting to some minor incident. You need to calm him or her down, discuss the situation and establish the facts. Later you might discuss the situation with the mentor and get his or her ideas. If the matter can't be resolved you need to discuss it with your own boss. When a new person is not suited to the job or

---

**UNIT/DEPARTMENT
INDUCTION INFORMATION CHECKLIST**

Introduction to the Organization and the Job
Action: Manager/Supervisor meets with the new person

Items covered might include:
- [ ] The unit/department 'mission', goals, and specific objectives
- [ ] Structure of the unit/department/organization(organization chart)
- [ ] Scale of the unit/department
  - staff numbers, facilities, budget, etc.
- [ ] Job description (general)
- [ ] How the new person's job fits in with that of others
- [ ] What is expected of the new person (general)
- [ ] Orientation schedule for first day and week
- [ ] Identification of key resource people
  in the unit/department, including the mentor
- [ ] List of staff names, jobs, and telephone numbers

Work Environment: Physical and Personal
*Action: Mentor provides a tour of the working area and introduces
the new person to the other members of staff*

Items covered might include:
- [ ] The unit/department working area
- [ ] The new person's working area
- [ ] Washrooms and lavatories
- [ ] Telephones -new person's number, internal/outside lines,
  switchboard, messages, etc.
- [ ] Photocopying equipment and access
- [ ] Computer equipment and access
- [ ] How to get supplies and equipment
- [ ] Canteen/dining facilities
- [ ] Car parking, travel arrangements
- [ ] Basic safety rules including no-smoking areas
- [ ] Restricted areas
- [ ] Accident procedures
- [ ] Protective clothing
- [ ] Fire exits and fire drills
- [ ] First aid and nursing facilities

Figure 2.2

Further Induction
Action: Manager/Supervisor provides review meetings

- [ ] Job description (detailed)
- [ ] Unit/department special projects and responsibilities - possible involvement of new person
- [ ] List of key resource people outside the unit/department
- [ ] Probationary period
- [ ] Performance appraisal scheme - what is expected of the person
- [ ] Training and development opportunities

COMPANY INDUCTION INFORMATION CHECKLIST
These items should have been covered by employment or personnel but you may need to check with the new person that the information has been covered and understood

Personnel policies and procedures
- [ ] Time keeping/recording - hours, breaks and lunch-time
- [ ] Pay: when and how
- [ ] Explanation of pay-slip
- [ ] Overtime
- [ ] Savings scheme
- [ ] Allowances
- [ ] Sick pay and who to call if sick
- [ ] Leave and holidays
- [ ] Pension schemes and life insurance
- [ ] Car and other expenses claims
- [ ] Disciplinary procedures
- [ ] Grievance procedures
- [ ] General rules, regulations and employee relations reference materials
- [ ] Department's special policies

Trade Unions and Employee Involvement
- [ ] Trade union membership or recognition policies
- [ ] Who's who: trade union representatives
- [ ] Joint consultative systems: quality circles, briefing groups, etc.
- [ ] Pay bargaining system: national and local agreements

Welfare and other Benefits
- [ ] Sports and social facilities
- [ ] Staff purchases
- [ ] Suggestions scheme
- [ ] Occupational health service
- [ ] Access to personal welfare counselling
- [ ] Mortgage assistance, loans

Figure 2.2 *(cont)*

organization, it may be better for both of you to find out sooner rather than later.

Action items

Using a matrix like the one shown in Figure 2.3, list five positive actions that you will take in order to improve the induction of new staff. Under 'person', identify the person or people responsible for taking action. Under 'dates', put start and completion dates.

ACTION ITEMS			
No.	Item	Person	Dates
1			
2			
3			
4			
5			

Figure 2.3

CHAPTER 3
How to Provide Mentoring and On-the-job Training

'I like to compare mentors and the mentoring process to sequoia trees. The sequoia grows to be hundreds of feet tall and lives for more than a thousand years. . . . By providing shelter and nutrition to neighbouring plants and animals, the sequoia contributes 80 per cent more to the forest environment than it takes. As people receive mentoring's benefits, they grow and achieve. They also develop roots in their organizations, and begin to mentor other achievers, thus giving back more than they received. But there's something else about sequoias and mentoring that carries equal importance, and it is so obvious that I missed it for years. A sequoia never stops growing. As long as it lives, it develops and contributes to everything around it. That is the real meaning of mentoring. . . .'. Jerry Willbur, *Training and Development Journal*, November 1987.*

The original Mentor appears in Homer's Greek classic, The Odyssey. *While Odysseus is away at the Trojan war, Mentor serves as a tutor and guide to Odysseus' son, Telemachus. The dictionary therefore describes a mentor as 'A close, trusted and experienced counsellor or guide'.*

In the work situation, mentoring involves deliberately pairing your skilled and experienced staff with less experienced people. This chapter is intended to help you set up a mentoring and job training system. It describes how you can use the skills of your experienced people to provide guidance and instruction for newer and less experienced staff. The specific objective is that you will identify mentors and set up a mentoring and on-the-job training system in your own department.

Your current situation

1. List some of the job training activities going on in your department at the moment.

2. Consider your staff in terms of their on-the-job training and development needs. You could use a matrix like the one shown in Figure 3.1. Based on your discussions with them, your observations, performance reviews, etc., identify what you think are their training and development needs. If you don't know their

STAFF TRAINING/DEVELOPMENT NEEDS	
Staff member	Needs

Figure 3.1

needs you might ask them. They could surprise you by telling you of needs you never knew existed.

Why mentoring and mentors are important

Mentoring is important because it provides a structured way for your people to train and help each other. Recently, mentoring has tended to be discussed mainly in terms of developing young managers and 'high flyers', but it can be used to develop any type of employee. As discussed in the previous chapter, mentoring can reduce the shock of entry for newcomers to the organization. It can also be used as a means of providing on-the-job training and coaching. In this way mentoring is similar to traditional apprenticeship training where the new recruit would be introduced to the job and work under the personal direction of a master craftsman.

The growth in informal and formal mentoring programmes is linked with a growing disenchantment with traditional education and training courses. These courses often seem too general, too dependent on classroom lecturing and too time-consuming. Often there's no follow-up after the courses to check that learning can be and is applied to the job.

Benefits of mentoring

What's in it for you
Mentoring can help you in the following ways.

- By allowing you to delegate some of your induction and staff training responsibilities to a skilled and experienced mentor.

- It develops positive attitudes and good work habits in new people. The mentor's attitudes towards the job and the organization – habits like punctuality and concern for quality work – can strongly influence the new or inexperienced employee. Personal contact with the mentor can also help the inexperienced employee establish personal and emotional ties to the organization.

- By reducing the danger of problems arising through a new person's ignorance of the organization. Through their mentors new people can learn directly about the business, company policies and procedures and gain organizational 'know-how'. Mentoring can also improve the work environment by encouraging mutual support and teamwork within your department.

- In providing job training and development where you need it and when you need it. Mentoring can be an alternative to sending someone away for training or waiting for a vacant 'slot' in a formal training course. It can also reduce the expenditure and time spent in travelling and attending formal training and development courses.

- By increasing the versatility of employees in your department through cross-training. Mentoring ensures that training is tailored to individual needs, fits the real job and can be done through regular work activities.

What's in it for the employee

Mentoring can help the new or inexperienced employee in the following ways.

- By providing an individual training programme. The mentor can judge whether the person is really learning and can change or tailor the training based on direct observation of the person's progress. The mentor's instruction, feedback and evaluation have a direct impact on performance.

- It involves the person actively. Mentoring is necessarily an active rather than a passive learning situation. The employee is provided with immediate and informal feedback on progress and can't hide at the back of a classroom.

- Through eliminating the distance between the learning situation and job performance. The 'transfer of learning' to the workplace is not a problem as it often is with classroom-based training.

● By providing reassurance and support for the new employee. As he or she gains technical competence and confidence, less supervision is required. At the end of mentoring process the employee should be no longer a learner but a peer and the relationship with the mentor should be one between equals.

What's in it for the mentor

As the quotation introducing this chapter emphasizes, the benefits of mentoring to the mentor are as important as the benefits to the employee being mentored. Mentoring can benefit the mentor in the following ways.

● By providing recognition for job expertise and experience. This recognition often helps mentors gain more confidence and a sense of pride and satisfaction through helping inexperienced employees grow and develop.

● It helps him or her become more skilled and knowledgeable in their own field. One way to become an expert in something is to train someone else how to do it. Involvement in training can also extend the mentor's knowledge and provide fresh ideas and perspectives.

● By providing assistance with his or her own work and allowing the mentor to work on new assignments. Career development involves staff taking on more responsibility and gaining new skills. Through mentoring, senior staff can gain more time for their own development and acquire leadership, instructional and coaching skills.

● It increases his or her motivation. Assigning mentoring responsibilities in itself is motivating to many employees and increases their self-esteem. For senior or middle level staff who have many years of experience, the mentoring role can revitalize their interest in work. The employee they are working with may provide some new perspectives and his or her enthusiasm for the job may revive the mentor's own motivation. In particular, the mentor may avoid 'burnout' by delegating some of the routine

MENTORING PROGRAMME GUIDELINES

PREPARATION

1. IDENTIFY A MENTORING NEED ☐

2. ASSESS WHETHER MENTORING WILL WORK ☐

3. SELECT THE MENTOR(S) ☐

4. MEET WITH THE MENTOR ☐

5. MEET WITH THE EMPLOYEE ☐

6. ARRANGE FOR MENTOR TRAINING ☐

MENTORING IMPLEMENTATION

1. ASSESS INDIVIDUAL NEEDS ☐

2. ON-THE-JOB TRAINING → COACHING → MONITORING ☐

3. ASSESS MENTORING RESULTS AND FURTHER NEEDS ☐

FOLLOW-UP

1. FOLLOW-UP ON INDIVIDUAL PROGRESS ☐

2. EVALUATE MENTORING PROGRAMME ☐

Figure 3.2

work and 'additional responsibilities' to the person they are mentoring.

Mentoring guidelines

If you are interested in mentoring, some basic steps in organizing a mentoring system are shown in Figure 3.2. These steps are shown in the form of a checklist to make them easy to use. The notes which follow describe each of these steps in turn and provide further information and suggestions on how to implement the steps.

Preparation
1. Identify whether there's need for mentoring
Look back to question 2 in 'Your Current Situation' at the beginning of this chapter. What training and developmental work activities should your staff participate in during the next year? What do your new people need to do? Who needs to learn a new skill? Who can teach particular skills?

2. Assess whether mentoring will work
Before you establish a mentoring system you need to look at your department and consider carefully whether mentoring is likely to succeed or not. Figure 3.3 lists some organizational factors which can lead to the success of a mentoring programme. Check whether these factors apply in your organization.

If one or more factors do not apply and you still want to start a mentoring system, think about how you can overcome these obstacles. For example, if there is a lack of management commitment, you or someone else might make a presentation on mentoring. If there are no rewards for mentoring, your organization might reward effective mentors through the performance review system.

3. Select the mentor(s)
A list of factors to consider in selecting mentors is shown in Figure 3.4. Don't be too demanding though. If you limit yourself

---

RECIPE FOR MENTORING SUCCESS

Here are some ingredients that can lead to the success of a mentoring system:

- There is a management commitment to make mentoring a success.
- There are rewards and organizational recognition for being a mentor.
- Experienced staff want to become mentors.
- Managers, supervisors and mentors are ready to behave as trainers and coaches rather than as evaluators, 'catching people out'.
- New and inexperienced staff are not afraid to ask for guidance.
- Potential mentors are well informed and good at their jobs. They instruct new employees in correct methods
- No more than two or three employees are assigned to a mentor at one time.

Figure 3.3

to people with *all* these characteristics, you might not have any mentors!

As you think about your staff, try to match your potential mentors and those who need to learn. The best matches occur between mentors and staff who share similar jobs and who work in close proximity to each other so they can easily get together. You might identify people who are already functioning as informal mentors – staff who already seem to have the motivation and some experience of mentoring. You might consider which of your senior staff might benefit from taking on mentoring responsibilities. Also, when you select mentors don't forget to include yourself, especially if you need to train a successor or someone to sit in for you.

MENTOR SELECTION

You should select as mentors staff who have:

- A positive attitude towards the job and good work habits.
- Good job skills – but they don't need to be the highest performers.
- Enough experience of the job and the organization to be effective and credible in the mentor's role.
- A willingness to help other people and respect for colleagues.
- Enough patience to train less experienced staff.
- Sensitivity to others' feelings. Mentors need to be tactful in giving feedback.
- Enough maturity to know that training and improvement takes time.

Figure 3.4

4. *Meet with the mentor*

Meet with the potential mentor and explain the purpose and benefits of mentoring. At the beginning you need to find out whether the person really wants to be a mentor. Not all experienced staff are willing to take the trouble to share their know-how. Indeed, some may enjoy the advantage that their superior knowledge gives them and withhold important information about the job. If you think this might be the case, either don't use the person as a mentor, or explain very clearly what is required and monitor the mentoring carefully.

You also need to elicit any concerns or fears that the prospective mentor might have. If these concerns are not discussed at the start, they can undermine the whole mentoring process. If the person is interested in being a mentor, help him or her to recognize their potential contribution – a little bit of flattery is useful here. Explain how the person might benefit from being a mentor – you might use the points under 'What's in it for the mentor'. Let the mentor know what support he or she will receive – manuals, materials, your own and other people's involvement. Indeed, your own interest and support is particularly important here, especially if the mentor lacks confidence and is uncertain of his or her role.

5. Meet with the employee
You should also meet with the person who is going to be mentored. Explain the purpose and benefits of mentoring and what the employee will learn. Mentoring involves people working together, a mutual exchange, and the employee should know that he or she is just as responsible for the success of mentoring as the mentor.

6. Arrange for mentor training
You can increase the chances of successful mentoring by arranging training for mentors in effective training techniques and how and when to apply skills such as coaching. Don't try to turn your mentors into sophisticated training people though. They may feel overwhelmed with all the things they seem to have to learn, lose confidence, and fail. Some organizations have set up large-scale mentoring programmes and provided training for mentors. This mentor training often consists of:

- a discussion of mentoring and the concerns the mentor(s) might have;
- an orientation to any training materials that will be used;
- information and practice in how to:
    prepare for mentoring sessions
    demonstrate a skill or a procedure
    coach an employee.

Mentoring implementation
The following information is intended to help you either in conducting mentoring sessions yourself or in observing and advising on these sessions.

Figure 3.2 identifies the main steps involved in the implementation of mentoring and shows how they are linked. Let's

ASSESSMENT OF NEED		
KNOWLEDGE OF TASK	EXPERIENCE OF TASK	METHODOLOGY
None	None	Train – Coach – Monitor
Some knowledge	Little or none	Coach (then if required, Train) – Monitor
Some previous knowledge	Some previous experience	Coach – Monitor
Substantial previous knowledge	Substantial previous experience	Monitor

Figure 3.5

consider each of these steps in turn and how they fit into the work situation.

1. Assess individual needs.
First of all the mentor assesses the employee's knowledge and skill level in a particular task. He or she considers what is needed for the employee to reach the required job standard. Clearly the methodology selected by a mentor depends on the employee's past knowledge and experience of the particular task. The matrix in Figure 3.5 indicates the appropriate methodology for a mentor to use relative to the employee's knowledge and experience.

2a. On-the-job training
Job training is appropriate when an employee has little or no knowledge or skill in a particular task. The mentor can act as a

trainer, explaining and demonstrating how to perform the unfamiliar task or procedure.

Demonstration is a key skill in job training The mentor may be an expert in performing the particular task but in order to transfer that expertise to another employee he or she needs to demonstrate effectively. However, demonstrations are often poorly conducted. Figure 3.6 lists some of the most common reasons for demonstrations being ineffective. How many of these apply in your department?

The most effective way of demonstrating how to do something is the Three-Step Demonstration Method. The steps are as follows:

STEP 1: The mentor explains and demonstrates how to do the task.

STEP 2: The employee explains how to do the task while the mentor demonstrates how to do the task again.

STEP 3: The employee explains and demonstrates how to do the task.

SOME REASONS FOR INEFFECTIVE DEMONSTRATION

- The employee can't see the demonstration properly.
- There is no clear objective – the employee isn't sure what he or she is supposed to do.
- The mentor hasn't stimulated interest or motivated the employee.
- The mentor speaks rapidly and does the demonstration too quickly.
- The mentor talks too much and doesn't ask questions or listen.
- The mentor is more concerned with demonstrating his or her own expertise than with training the employee.

Figure 3.6

This method has many practical advantages:

- It combines speaking with seeing and doing. The employee is actively involved in each step and this makes it more likely that learning will take place.
- The employee sees the demonstration twice. In many demonstrations the employee sees the task performed only once and then practises. As a result, misunderstandings can arise, there's confusion and the employee can feel embarrassed and frustrated.
- There is a mental rehearsal and reinforcement through the employee 'telling' in Step 2. Mental rehearsal is a good predictor of success in many fields.
- The mentor knows whether the employee has really understood before he or she starts to try. This provides a safeguard against accidents. In situations where safety is a priority, Step 2 may be repeated.
- Feedback is given at each step of the demonstration.

In some situations – for example, where production needs to be maintained or complex equipment assembled or broken down – the Three-Step Method may take too much time or be too disruptive. The following sequence might then be used:

STEP 1: The mentor explains and demonstrates how to do the task.

STEP 2: The employee does the task and the mentor coaches.

STEP 3: The employee does the task and the mentor monitors.

Demonstration preparation form
The Demonstration Preparation Form, Figure 3.7, will help your mentors to prepare for training sessions where a demonstration is required. The notes below explain how to use the form.

Date
If you have a choice of dates, decide what is the best date for this specific demonstration.

DEMONSTRATION PREPARATION FORM

Date:_____Session time:_____
Place: _____
Demonstration task:_____
_____

Equipment/materials required:_____
_____

Visual aids/handouts required:_____
_____
_____

References:_____
_____

Introduction
Session objective(s). By the end of this
demonstration, the employee will be able to:

_____
_____
_____
_____

*Make sure the objective(s) state employee
performance. Any particular conditions or standards
need to be included. Make your objective clear and
memorable through the use of a visual aid.*

Visual aid: _____
Explanation of how objective(s) relates to employee's
job and interests - what's in it for the employee:

_____
_____
_____
_____
Time for introduction:_____

Figure 3.7

64

DEMONSTRATION PREPARATION FORM

Explanation of the task and demonstration of each step. *Include visual aids/handouts that support and highlight main steps. Task steps in sequence:*

1._____
2._____
3._____
4._____
5._____
6._____
7._____
8._____
9._____

Rehearse these demonstration steps. Have you missed out any small but important steps? Are there any safety factors the employee(s) should be aware of?

Questions to involve employee(s) and check understanding:

_____
_____
_____

Employee(s) explained and trainer showed the steps:

_____

Check and reinforce main points in each step of the demonstration.

Employee(s) explained and showed the steps:

_____

Time for demonstration:_____

Practice/Evaluation
Practice/Evaluation activity:_____

_____
_____

Time for practice/evaluation:_____

Figure 3.7 *(cont)*

Session time
Before you decide the time and length of the session, consider the objective(s) and your demonstration plan. How long will it take for the employee to learn this task? You may need to arrange for several sessions.

Place
If you have a choice of sites, decide which is the best for an effective session. Where will noise, distractions or likelihood of interruption be at a minimum? If you are using a training room or office, book the room in advance.

Demonstration task
Briefly describe the task.

Equipment/materials required.
List any equipment or materials you need for the demonstration. If more than one employee is participating, try to ensure that there is enough equipment or materials for everyone. Check that any equipment you will use has been tested and that all functions are working properly. If safety is a factor, make sure that the appropriate clothing, eg gloves, helmets, is available for yourself and the employee.

Visual aids/handouts required.
Identify any visual aids, eg overhead transparencies, or handouts you will need. Remember, a writing pad on the table serves the same purpose for the mentor as the flipchart does for those who teach groups. A simple diagram can help make your explanation much clearer.

References.
List any manuals or textbooks you will use or refer to. Ensure that these are available if needed and mark any specific references so that the employee can easily find them. Decide whether you need to give copies of the reference material to the employee.

Introduction

Staff who have not received trainer training often jump into delivering the technical content of training without introducing their material. The result is that the employee becomes confused at the beginning and gets lost in a cloud of technical data and jargon. Your introduction should not take up a great amount of time, but the investment of a few minutes in getting the employee off on the right foot is well worthwhile.

Session objective(s).
Make sure the objective(s) state an employee performance. Any particular conditions or standards need to be included.

Visual aid.
Make your objective clear and memorable through the use of a visual aid. If possible, show an example of the completed work or the end-product of the task before giving the demonstration. People are more likely to be successful when they can see what the result of their work looks like.

Explanation of how the objective(s) relates to the employee's job and interests – what's in it for the employee.
Explain the importance of the task. Why is it done? How does it relate to other tasks the employee has learned? How critical is it? What will happen if there's a mistake? How frequently does the task need to be done?

Time for introduction.
Estimate how much time you really need. Be generous to allow for questions or any further explanation. If new terms and technical language are involved, explain these in the introduction.

Demonstration

Explanation of the task and demonstration of each step.
Before you begin your demonstration, ensure that the employee will be able see everything clearly. This is particularly important when you are showing small objects or operations. Sometimes it

may be necessary to stand back from the job to let the employee see, or exaggerate movements to demonstrate the correct way to do something.

Task steps in sequence.
Break the task down into specific steps. These steps might be listed on a handout so that the employee can follow the steps easily and use the handout for individual practice and later as a job aid. If there are a number of employees involved in the demonstration, the steps might also be listed on an overhead transparency or flipchart. Make sure there are no gaps or steps missed out in the task. Experienced people often forget to mention the small transitional steps which are vital if the employee is to get it right. In this first demonstration you should be rather slow and deliberate in explaining and demonstrating the steps.

As part of your preparation, rehearse these demonstration steps. Are there any safety factors the employee(s) should be aware of?

Questions to involve employee(s) and check understanding.
List the questions you might ask if you feel the employee is 'losing track' or interest in the demonstration. Questioning is particularly important when your explanation/demonstration is lengthy or technically complex. Remember, questioning increases involvement and the chances that the employee will retain the information.

Have employee(s) explain as you show the steps OR have employee(s) explain and show the steps one at a time while you coach.
Your second demonstration and the 'mental rehearsal' of the employee 'telling' the steps are particularly valuable, especially where safety factors are involved. If the employee demonstrates at this stage, provide coaching and feedback. Check and reinforce the main points and look out for any signs that the employee is not clear on something or has difficulty with a specific step.

Have employee(s) explain and show the steps.
Again, speaking is combined with seeing and doing. The employee should show only one step at a time to reduce the possibility of error. Getting it right first time will increase the person's confidence and reduce the risk of problems later on. Coach as required.

Time for demonstration.
Estimate how much time you really need for all the steps. Be generous to allow for questions or any further demonstration.

Practice/evaluation
Practice/evaluation activity.
If you have more than one employee, ensure that everyone is involved in the practice activity and no one is neglected. Monitor the practice and coach as required.

Time for practice/evaluation.
Based upon the employee's level of success, decide how much time is needed for mastery. Practice time should be more than just a few minutes at the end of the session and the employee should have time to perform the task more than once. Avoid the common mistake of sacrificing practice time for 'more explanation'.

2b. Coaching.
Usually not even a new employee needs to be trained in everything. Through coaching the mentor can provide guidance and give advice on tasks which the employee may know about and have done several times before, but which he or she needs more practice and experience with.

For more detailed information on coaching techniques, turn to Chapter 9 on how to coach your people.

2c. Monitoring.
When an employee has knowledge and some experience of the task but needs more practice, the mentor can monitor his or her performance. The mentor needn't stand over the employee when

69

he or she is doing the job, but observes so that advice and support can be provided if needed. Monitoring often involves delegation (see Chapter 8 on delegation) where the mentor identifies a task, gives the employee some instructions, assists where necessary and then follows-up on the task when it is completed. The mentor then needs to assess whether any further training or coaching is needed, or whether the employee can be given another task.

3. Assess mentoring results and further needs.
Through observation and discussion with the mentor and the employee you can assess the results and decide whether further mentoring is needed.

Follow-up

1. Follow-up on individual progress.
In formal on-the-job training programmes the personnel or training staff might keep track of the administrative details like how many units of a course or tasks the employee has completed or how many hours it took to complete a unit.

Your follow-up on the mentoring sessions is more important though, as you can assist and provide support where necessary. This follow-up should involve discussions with the mentor and employee. Both you and the mentor also need to keep track of how much time the mentor spent with the employee.

Your follow-up may also involve some observation of mentoring sessions, perhaps using the Demonstration Checklist.

2. Evaluate mentoring programme.
After a period of time you should evaluate the success of mentoring in your department. In their New Employee Mentor Programme, 3M evaluates the mentoring assignment after six months. Each mentor, the employee being mentored and the employee's supervisor complete an evaluation questionnaire. If you decide to evaluate your mentoring programme, here are some questions you might consider:

- Why specifically do you need to evaluate the programme? Do you need an evaluation to justify mentoring, to identify any strengths and weaknesses in the programme, to extend the programme? Your reasons for conducting an evaluation and their degree of urgency will determine how much money, time and effort you spend on evaluation and the methods you use.
- What will you do with the results of the evaluation? Will they be sent to upper management, publicized in the organization?
- Why did you start the mentoring programme? What did you want it to achieve? For example, did you expect a positive effect in areas like turnover, employee skills, flexibility of staff, motivation of employees and mentors, readiness for higher responsibility?
- How would you define success for the mentoring programme?
- What data do you need to make decisions about the future of the programme?
- How can you best gather the data? Through interviews, questionnaires, computer print-outs on turnover, etc.?
- What reporting will you need from the mentors, employees, employees' supervisors?

Demonstration checklist

The checklist shown in Figure 3.8 can be used as a self-check by the mentor or as an observation tool by a manager or supervisor observing a demonstration. Note how each step is tied to the achievement of learning.

Common situations

Situation: There isn't enough time for mentoring in my department.
Response: There never is enough time! Yet there always seems to be time for people to make mistakes, revise, do it again and generally muddle through. If your operation is going to improve there has to be time for new and inexperienced staff to learn to do things correctly and get the basics right.

DEMONSTRATION CHECKLIST	
1.	Ensure that employee(s) can clearly see your demonstration
2.	State demonstration objective(s) and if applicable show the end-product
3.	Stimulate employee(s) interest – what's in it for me
4.	Avoid the mirror image or other visual distractions in the demonstration
5.	Explain and show each separate step in the task/ process
6.	Show the steps again and have employee(s) explain each step OR have the employee(s) explain and show the steps one at a time while you coach
7.	Ask questions to involve employee(s) and check their understanding
8.	Have employee(s) explain and show the steps one at a time
9.	Provide constructive feedback to employee(s)
10.	Provide sufficient practice time
11.	Ensure all employees are involved in the practice
12.	Assess employee(s) performance/end product and repeat steps or coach as necessary

Figure 3.8

Situation: The mentor is afraid that this new person will replace him or her. Mentoring seems a threat rather than an opportunity.

Response: Explain to the mentor how he or she is developing a new role. The mentor's knowledge and experience are being used and he or she is moving onto broader tasks. When someone is chosen as a mentor this can be motivating especially if you provide some special recognition or training for the new responsibility. For example, you might send the mentor on a trainer training or coaching course; mentoring might be mentioned in the organization's newsletter; or recognized through the performance review system.

Situation: The mentor isn't clear on the differences between mentoring and training. He or she feels like a teacher and always wants to train the employee. As a result, the employee feels that his or her existing knowledge and skills are being discounted.

Response: Together with the mentor, look at some of the tasks the person needs to learn. Based on this person's past knowledge and experience, identify those tasks where training, coaching or monitoring might be required. You might use the matrix in Figure 3.5 for this. Then discuss how the mentor might provide coaching and monitoring assistance instead of training.

Situation: The person being mentored seems to reject assistance and the mentor sees this as an unrewarding responsibility.

Response: Discuss the purposes of mentoring with the mentor and separately with the person being mentored. Don't get involved in any personality disputes but focus on the mentoring task and the employee's performance. If necessary, change the mentor.

Situation: One of your managers or supervisors is not a mentor. He lacks understanding or interest in mentoring and fails to provide time or support for mentoring.

Response: Explain the purposes and benefits of mentoring and identify the manager's or supervisor's particular responsibilities. These responsibilities may include: selecting mentors; orienting the mentors and the employees; monitoring progress; and generally supporting the mentoring process.

Situation: The employee expects to be promoted as a result of mentoring.
Response: To prevent the employee having unrealistic expectations, it's important for you to clearly communicate to him or her what participation in mentoring means – and what it does not mean. As a result of mentoring, the employee may gain additional information and skills. This will make him or her better equipped to do their present job and may also increase their 'promotability'. Promotion, however, often depends on other factors like the availability of posts, experience requirements and the situation inside the organization.

Action items

1. Using Figure 3.9, list your existing members of staff. What

PAIRING MENTORS AND EMPLOYEES		
STAFF MEMBER/ MENTOR	SKILL	PERSON NEEDING THE SKILL

Figure 3.9

could each of them teach other members of staff, especially new or inexperienced people joining your department or unit?

2. Choose one of the pairs you have linked, using the table in Figure 3.9. What problems may arise which could affect the success of the mentoring process? Identify three problems and a strategy for dealing with each:

Problem:

Strategy:

Problem:

Strategy:

Problem:

Strategy:

Use this as part of your preparation for meeting the mentor and the employee.

CHAPTER 4

How to Prepare for a Group Training Session

'To teach is to learn twice'. Joseph Joubert, *Pensees* (1842)

Employee training is too important an activity to be left just to 'trainers'. Indeed you can gain as much from training your staff as they can gain through learning from 'the boss'. By training others you can learn more about the overall operation, become more skilled and knowledgeable in the topic area and gain new perspectives on the job. You can also learn more about your employees and improve your own communication skills. This chapter will help you and your staff prepare for group training sessions. Even if you yourself are not training, the chapter will help you understand and support your 'trainers' and give them constructive feedback on their training sessions. Much of the information and many of the suggestions will also prove useful when you need to prepare a general business presentation or management briefing.

Your current situation

The purpose of training is learning and learning takes place more readily in some circumstances than in others. Figure 4.1 contains a list of ten factors which increase employee learning and the likelihood that group training will be successful. Consider the training in your department and check whether these statements apply. If a statement only partially applies, put a question mark (?). If a statement is not applicable, put N/A.

FACTORS OF TRAINING SUCCESS		
ITEM	STATEMENT	
1.	Group training sessions are given in response to specific job needs	
2.	Trainers are knowledgeable, enthusiastic and interested in training	
3.	Employees learn in a relaxed and constructive atmosphere	
4.	Training sessions have specific objectives which are stated at the beginning of the session	
5.	Employees' previous knowledge and experience is recognized and used	
6.	Training focuses on relevant and realistic problems and the practical application of learning	
7.	Employees participate in a variety of practice activities during training sessions	
8.	Trainers give sufficient time for new information to be discussed and for new skills to be practised	
9.	Employees' performance after training is evaluated and they have a sense of progress	
10.	Trainers follow-up to provide help and ensure that employees can apply what they have learnt	

Figure 4.1

Look at the factors you have marked with a ? or N/A. What might you do to improve the training situation in your department?

Why it's important for you to train

From the organizational point of view, the way to get training taken seriously and ensure its effectiveness is to use managers and supervisors as part-time 'trainers'. They are the people best qualified to provide training relevant to employees' needs and are in the best position to follow-up when people get back to the job.

Training is also one of the most valuable activities a manager or supervisor can be involved in. For example, you might want to give four separate hours of training to your group – one hour on some new procedures, one hour on job safety and two hours on how to use a new computer system. For each hour of actual training time three hours of preparation might be needed – a total expenditure of 16 hours of your time. Say you have 10 employees in your group. Next year they will work a total of about 18000 hours for your organization. If your training produces only a 5 per cent improvement in your employees' performance, your organization will gain the equivalent of 900 hours of work. This will be the result of 16 hours of your time and 40 hours of your employees' time – a total expenditure of 56 hours. The training profit would be 844 hours.

Through training, managers and supervisors also learn more about the problems that face employees and what the possible solutions are. Real problems can be discussed in training sessions and acted on as a result of feedback from employees. Organizations also benefit through the increased expertise of managers and supervisors who do some training. In order to train they must become more familiar with the organization's products, technology and services.

Through training, managers and supervisors also gain more contact with new employees entering the organization. They can help 'shape' the new employees and serve as role models.

Finally, training sessions conducted by managers and supervisors may be less polished than those from professional trainers but can result in more learning and impact on the total organization. Indeed, involving managers and supervisors in training can convert a training effort into an organization development effort that improves the overall health of the organization.

Benefits

What's in it for you
Managers and supervisors who act as trainers often learn more from the experience than participants do. By preparing and conducting training sessions you can achieve the following.

- Increase your knowledge and skill in the specific topic area. The best way to learn something thoroughly is to try and teach it.
- Develop your skills in group leadership. Through training you can increase your communication skills and confidence in dealing with your staff and with the people above you. In particular, conducting training sessions can improve your general presentation skills and the 'influencing skills' you need for meetings and management briefings.
- Gain a better understanding of what can be achieved in a classroom environment. You will be better equipped to select and assess off-the-job training courses for your employees.

What's in it for employees
When the manager or supervisor conducts training sessions, employees can do the following.

- Gain the knowledge and skills necessary to operate new equipment and work systems.
- Benefit from knowledge that comes 'straight from the source'. In particular, employees can learn more about the expectations and standards of the organization and their management.
- Discuss and give feedback on real work problems. At your group training sessions employees should be able to make

TRAINING PREPARATION GUIDELINES

VERIFY THE NEED

IDENTIFY THE TRAINER(S)

PREPARE THE TRAINING SESSION

1. PLAN FOR THE SESSION ☐
2. DEVELOP THE INTRODUCTION ☐
3. DEVELOP THE TRAINING PRESENTATION ☐
4. PREPARE HANDOUTS AND VISUAL AIDS ☐
5. DEVELOP APPLICATION/PRACTICE ACTIVITIES ☐
6. DEVELOP EVALUATION AND REVIEW ACTIVITIES ☐

REHEARSE AND TROUBLE-SHOOT YOUR TRAINING SESSION

Figure 4.2

suggestions and present their ideas on how problems might be solved.

- Benefit from there being no problem of 'learning transfer'. The training environment and work environment are the same so it's easier for employees to use what they've learned.
- Share expertise and experience through question and answer and discussion sessions with colleagues. This can be very effective if you make sure that communication in your training sessions is three-way:

    Manager or supervisor ————————►Employees
    Employees ————————► Manager or supervisor
    Employees ◄———————————► Employees

Training preparation guidelines

Preparation is vital in any kind of training and thorough preparation will help ensure the success of your group training sessions. This is as true for experienced trainers as it is for people who are new to training. The training preparation guidelines, Figure 4.2, can save you trying to remember things, stop you from missing out important steps and ensure that everything is prepared for your training session. Thorough preparation will also make you feel more confident at the start of a session and help you create a relaxed but businesslike training environment. Let us look at the preparation steps on the checklist in more detail.

Verify the need for group training
Ask yourself, 'Is a group training session needed?' It may be useful to get everyone together at the same time to give the new information or practise the new skills. There are significant advantages in ensuring that everyone is 'singing from the same sheet'. If there is a visiting expert, arranging for everyone to attend the same training session is also particularly cost-effective.

Identify the trainer(s)
If a group of employees needs to learn something and it's more

effective for them to learn together, you should look for an appropriate trainer or trainers.

Ask yourself, 'Who is the best person to give this training?' Is it your most experienced person, is it the person with the best communication skills, should it be yourself? Whoever it is, the guidelines below will help them to prepare for the session.

Prepare the training session
Use the Training Preparation Form, Figure 4.3, to prepare group training sessions. Don't be afraid to make changes on this preparation form or be too concerned with its appearance. The form is for you alone so treat it as a working outline and move backwards and forwards between pages. The main points of your presentation will affect your introduction; the practice activity or evaluation you choose will affect what you focus on in your presentation. Don't be afraid to revise and adjust your material as you develop your session.

Here are some suggestions on how to use this form.

1. Plan for the session

Topic.
Identify your training topic as clearly and as specifically as possible. Don't try to cover too many topics or one big topic in the session. The purpose of training is for employees to learn, not for you to present as much information as possible or cover material as quickly as possible.

Employee information – number of employees, previous knowledge/experience, ways to interest them in topic, etc.
Write down what you know about the employees who will attend this session. Ask yourself what they already know – are some of them completely new to this topic or do some of them know quite a lot already? What might particularly interest them? Your employees' previous knowledge, experience or interests tell you where to start from and what you might use as a springboard to move into your session.

TRAINING PREPARATION FORM

1. Plan for the session

Topic:_____

_____

Employee information - number, employees' previous
knowledge/experience of topic, ways to interest them
in topic, etc:_____

_____

_____

_____

_____

_____

Tools/equipment required:_____

_____

_____

_____

Job materials required:_____

_____

References:_____

_____

Date, time and length of training session:_____

_____

_____

Site of training session:_____

_____

_____

Figure 4.3

TRAINING PREPARATION FORM

2. Develop the Introduction
Session training objectives
Performance: *Employees will be able to*_____

_____

Conditions: *Given*_____

_____

Standard:_____

Visual aid: _____

What's in it for employees:_____

_____

_____

Questions to elicit employees' previous knowledge/
experience of topic: _____

_____

_____

_____

_____

Introduction time: _____

3.Develop the training presentation: main points

1. _____
2. _____
3. _____
4. _____
5. _____
6. _____
7. _____
8. _____
9. _____

Figure 4.3 *(cont)*

Questions to involve employees and check
understanding:_____
_____
_____
_____

Possible employee questions: _____
_____
_____
_____

Trainer presentation time: _____

4.Prepare handouts and visual aids

_____
_____
_____
_____
_____

5.Develop application/practice activities

_____
_____
_____
_____

Application/practice time: _____

6.Develop evaluation/review activites

_____
_____
_____
_____

Evaluation/review time: _____

Figure 4.3 *(cont)*

Tools/equipment required.
The number of employees will tell you how many tools or pieces of equipment you need. Can each person have something to practise with, or do they need to work in pairs or groups?

Job materials required.
Identify what employees will need to bring along with them – tools, equipment, manuals. Will safety clothing be required?

References.
List the job manuals, company procedures, training handbooks, that you and the employees will use or refer to. Identify which particular sections and pages employees will need to use. Then decide whether you will photocopy the appropriate reference materials, bring along the manuals and mark the appropriate entries or get the employees to practise finding the information themselves.

Date, time and length of training session.
Select a date based on the job situation and how long it will take you to prepare for the training session. Then ask yourself, 'When is the best time for employees to have this type of training?' 'Early morning, afternoon, Monday, Friday?' 'How long will it take them to learn this information or skill?' When you decide the time and length of the session, remember that learning requires employee involvement and practice. That takes time. If employees need several sessions you might assign a specific number of days to training or the time may be broken up into sessions of one day per week, two hours a day, every afternoon for two weeks, etc.

Site of training session.
If you have a choice of sites, decide which is most appropriate for this specific session and topic. Which site has the equipment you need or is easiest for you to bring the equipment to? Which site is easiest for people to get to? Where will there be least noise, distractions, or likelihood of interruptions from phones, tea trolleys or reverberations from the machine shop?

Book the room and then confirm it closer to the date of the training session.

2. Develop the introduction

Session training objective(s).
Write down the objective(s) for this training session. To do this ask yourself, 'What do I want them to be able to do by the end of this session?'

Your objective(s) should have three parts:

a. PERFORMANCE: What your employees should be able to do as a result of the training – their own performance and not what you will cover in the training session.

b. CONDITIONS: It will help you to plan your session if you also include in the objective any particular 'given' conditions. These may describe the 'cue' for the task – 'given a materials request' or 'given a faulty engine'.

The conditions may also describe the equipment, materials or manuals that employees will use to perform the task.

c. STANDARDS: You can measure the results of training more effectively if you specify standards – the level of speed, accuracy or acceptability that you expect the employees to reach by the end of training. If you have no standard or your standard is 'to the satisfaction of the manager or supervisor', think carefully about the level of speed, accuracy, frequency or other qualities you want. Then let your employees know your standard in your statement of the objective(s).

Model your objective(s) on the examples given in Figure 4.4.

When you have identified your objective(s) ask yourself, 'Am I being too ambitious?', 'Is there enough time for employees to practise and to achieve the objective(s)?' If you have several objectives, it might be best to deal with them in separate training sessions. If you have one broad objective, you should break it down into several specific objectives which again might be dealt with in several training sessions.

STANDARDS FOR MEASURING TRAINING EFFECTIVENESS			
	PERFORMANCE	CONDITIONS	STANDARD
1.	Each employee will be able to adjust all valves on the X engine	Given: A faulty engine, a feeler gauge and a standard set of tools	In accordance with instruction manual
2.	Each trainee nurse will be able to attach a patient to a telemetry monitor	Given: A heart patient, three EKG electrodes and a telemetry monitor	A clear picture within five minutes
3.	Each assistant will be able to answer all customer questions on the new range of products	Given: Customer questions and the product range booklet as a reference	To customer's satisfaction and in accordance with product range booklet

Figure 4.4

Visual aid.
Make your objective(s) clear and memorable by producing a transparency or flipchart page which states the objective(s).

What's in it for employees.
This is the motivational part of the introduction, the most neglected and yet potentially the most critical part of a training session. Write down some statements which you can use to explain why employees need this training and what they can gain from your session. Alternatively, think of some questions which you can ask to elicit from employees the relevance of the

objective(s) to their jobs. You may regard 'what's in it for employees' as self-evident – they've got to learn this to do the job or to become better qualified. But if employees know specifically how this training will help them, how critical this is or how frequently it arises, then they are much more likely to want to learn. If you can't say 'what's in it for the employees' and describe the benefits of your training session, don't go ahead with it.

Questions to elicit employees' previous knowledge/experience of the topic.
Write down some questions you can use to find out what employees know about this topic. For example, 'How many of you have experienced this problem before?', or 'Has anyone had training in this area before?' Make sure you start from a firm foundation and what the employees already know. By asking these questions you also show respect for your employees' previous knowledge and experience and a willingness to discuss and harness it in the interests of the group.

The time for your introduction should be about 10 per cent of your total session time.

3. Develop the training presentation

A presentation should have an introduction, a body which gives the main information and a review or conclusion. When you outline your training session it's often best to begin with the body to establish your main ideas. You can't write an effective introduction until you know the main points in your session.

To help you produce an outline here are some questions you might ask yourself.

● 'What are the most important points in my presentation?' Try to keep the number of main ideas to a minimum. The average person tends to remember things in small groups with three as the ideal number. You might have three main points in your presentation with three or four sub-points under each main heading. In visual terms this would produce four overhead transparencies or slides with three or four points on each. The first transparency or slide would be an overview listing the three main points.

- 'Which of these points should I emphasize most?' People tend to remember best the first and last things they see or hear in a training session. Keep this in mind when you think of your sequence of points and what needs to be emphasized in your introduction and conclusion.

- 'What might they have difficulty with and what will we need to spend more time on?' Respond to employee needs by concentrating on the information or skills which they may have difficulty with. Provide additional explanation and use familiar examples to illustrate technical concepts. Provide more discussion or practice when employees experience difficulty.

- 'Does all this fit together logically?', 'Have I missed out any small but important points?' For example, are there any safety factors the employees should be aware of? Put yourself in the employees' place and look at your plan critically as an outsider. Then improve it.

Finally, review your outline and decide where you can most effectively use visual aids. Make the cues for visual aids stand out in your plan by highlighting them with underlining, capitalization, colour or other visual prompts.

Questions to involve employees and check understanding.
List some questions you might ask to increase participation, ensure that employees understand what you are saying or showing to them, or to trigger brief discussions.

Possible employee questions.
List the questions that employees might ask, not only during a question and answer session, but during the training session itself. Be prepared to answer these questions.

Trainer presentation time.
Estimate how long it will take you to give the presentation.

4. Prepare handouts and visual aids
Studies of business communication have shown that visual aids

significantly increase a presenter's persuasiveness. Speakers using visual aids are seen as being better prepared, more professional, clearer and more interesting, than speakers who do not use visuals. This is because visual aids generate interest and provide a change of pace: they capture people's attention. When they are used in training, visual aids increase people's retention of information and learning.

You should therefore support your training session with visual aids that add variety, highlight your key points and provide a clear structure for your presentation. Visual aids will also help you deal with your nervousness because they give your audience something to look at in addition to you.

Visual aids, however, are not a simple recipe for success. They need to be appropriate and used effectively to:

- Increase the impact of your message. Your visual aids should focus on key words and ideas and reduce confusion or the possibility of misunderstanding.
- Present information concisely and clarify the relationship between ideas, parts of equipment or the stages in a process.
- Summarize, organize and help the audience think through your presentation.

Finally your visual aids should be *visual*. Trainers often develop visual aids with too much information on them. For suggestions on how to develop handouts, flipcharts, overhead transparencies and slides see the Appendix at the end of this book.

Visual equipment required.
List any equipment you will need to show your visual aids – overhead projector, slide projector or video recorder and monitor. Decide where you will get this equipment.

5. Develop application/practice activities
How much employees learn is directly proportional to their involvement in the training and the practice they get. Identify activities you can use so that employees can apply or practise what they have learned.

In a training sequence practice comes after presentation but remember the 20 minute rule! The average adult can only listen with retention for 20 minutes so avoid situations where you have to speak for long periods of time. If you have a long presentation, break it up with discussion, group activities, video, question and answer sessions or practice activities. Add variety and increase involvement in your training by integrating your presentation and the employees' practice activities as closely as possible.

In particular, use group activities where employees discuss a question or work on a task in groups. They can then report their findings to the whole group. Group activities also have the advantage that you are 'off-stage' and can go round the groups giving advice and coaching when required.

For example, if you are conducting a session for supervisors on the company's personnel policies and procedures, instead of lecturing on the personnel manuals you might ask the participants to identify some common situations and problem areas. Then divide the supervisors into small groups, give them copies of the manuals and let them work on finding answers to these situations and problem areas. Each group might work on different situations or problems or a 'mix' of the same and different ones. Then when the groups report at the end of the activity they can learn from each other. Certainly, people remember and learn more from what they find out themselves than from what they are told.

Application/practice time.
Estimate the time you need to provide sufficient practice for employees to achieve the objective(s).

6. Develop evaluation and review activities
Decide how you can measure what employees have learnt. You might use a quiz, a group activity or a hands-on task.

Finally, review the objectives of your training session and the main points. You might ask employees to write down three things they have learned from your session or one important thing they will apply back on the job. Then ask each person to give their answers.

Evaluation review time.
Based on your activities, estimate how long evalualism/review will take. Between 5 and 10 per cent of the total session time is usual.

Action items

Training effectiveness is closely linked to the confidence that comes from practice. Rehearse your training session with friends and let them give you feedback using the Feedback Form shown in Figure 4.5. Note that it is possible to put a check mark in both the 'Good' and 'Needs Work' boxes. For example, there might be some good visuals and some that need improvement. Your audience should use a question mark (?) if an activity should appear but doesn't, and N/A for not applicable. In the 'Comments/Suggestions' section, strengths as well as suggestions for improvement should be noted.

When you practise, you might record your voice to develop your vocal skills. Even better you might use video. Practice with video feedback not only improves people's training and presentation skills dramatically, but increases their confidence and willingness to speak.

TRAINING FEEDBACK FORM

Trainer's name:_____

Training objective as stated:

_____

_____

PERFORMANCE	GOOD	NEEDS WORK	COMMENTS/ SUGGESTIONS
1. Stated session objective(s) clearly, including employee action(s), any conditions, and the standard(s) required			
2. Explained how the objective(s) related to employee jobs and interests - What's In It For Me			
3. Elicited employees' previous knowledge / experience related to training topic			
4. Explained main points of the training session clearly and in logical sequence			
5. Used visual aids - handouts / flipchart / transparencies / slides / video - effectively to highlight main points			
6. Used questions to involve employees and check understanding			
7. Encouraged employees' own questions / comments			

Figure 4.5

TRAINING FEEDBACK FORM

Trainer's name: _____

Training objective as stated:

_____

_____

PERFORMANCE	GOOD	NEEDS WORK	COMMENTS/ SUGGESTIONS
8. Used appropriate delivery skills: • Interest/enthusiasm shown • Eye contact - all employees • Gestures and movement - natural • Voice - loud enough, pace and tone vary, pauses used • Language - understandable, no jargon or slang			
9. Provided enough time to apply / practise new information			
10. Used an evaluation tool and / or reviewed the session with employees			

Presentation strengths : _____

_____

_____

_____

_____

Additional comments / suggestions: _____

_____

_____

_____

_____

Figure 4.5 *(cont)*

CHAPTER 5

How to Conduct a Group Training Session

> What I hear, I forget
> What I see, I remember
> What I do, I understand
>
> *Confucius, 451 BC.*

Keep this quotation in mind when you are conducting a group training session or giving a presentation. When you tell people something, that doesn't mean they are learning. When you show them something – demonstrate a skill or use visual aids to explain a process – there is more chance of employees remembering it. And when your staff can discuss and apply new information or practise new skills, they are more likely to understand and learn.

This chapter will help you conduct an effective training session – one from which your employees learn. Much of the information and many of the suggestions will also prove useful when you need to give a general business presentation or briefing.

Your current situation

Look at the feedback you received on your rehearsal or dry run. Then list the suggestions you might follow and the improvements you need to make in the following areas:

Introduction and objectives:

Presentation content:

Handouts and visual aids:

Application/practice activities:

Evaluation/review activities:

List the things you should do to improve your training presentation skills:

Conducting a training session - guidelines

The guidelines in Figure 5.1 provide a checklist of things to do when you are making your final preparations and conducting a training session. The notes below explain and give suggestions on how you might use the guidelines.

Final preparations

1. Prepare employees.
It helps training to get off to a good start if you personally contact employees and confirm the date, time and location of the training session. Confusion over times and location can disrupt the beginning of your session, embarrass late-comers and lead them to make a poor start. Other reasons for this personal contact are to spark employees' interest, assign any pre-training tasks and sometimes to tell them to bring along work materials.

Letting employees know about the course beforehand also alerts you to, and can reduce any problems caused by, differences between the training objectives and what employees expect. You may also use this pre-training contact to emphasize that they will be active participants in the training session.

CONDUCTING A TRAINING SESSION - GUIDELINES

FINAL PREPARATIONS

1. PREPARE EMPLOYEES ☐
2. PREPARE YOURSELF ☐
3. PREPARE TRAINING AREA AND EQUIPMENT ☐
4. HARNESS YOUR NERVOUS ENERGY ☐

CONDUCT THE SESSION

1. STATE SESSION OBJECTIVE(S) ☐
2. RELATE OBJECTIVE(S)
   TO EMPLOYEE JOBS/INTERESTS ☐
3. ELICIT EMPLOYEES' PREVIOUS
   KNOWLEDGE/EXPERIENCE ☐
4. PRESENT MAIN POINTS OF SESSION ☐
5. USE VISUAL AIDS TO HIGHLIGHT MAIN POINTS ☐
6. USE QUESTIONS TO INVOLVE EMPLOYEES AND
   CHECK UNDERSTANDING ☐
7. ENCOURAGE EMPLOYEE QUESTIONS/COMMENTS ☐
8. USE APPROPRIATE DELIVERY SKILLS ☐
9. PROVIDE TIME FOR APPLICATION/PRACTICE ☐
10. EVALUATE/REVIEW THE SESSION ☐

Figure 5.1

2. Prepare yourself.

Once you have made arrangements for the training session and prepared your materials, you need to ensure that *you* are fully prepared. The day before the session, check your preparation form, handouts and any visual aids you will use. This is vital, particularly if you are conducting a course away from your own work site.

To ensure you don't forget anything you will need for the training session, use the Materials Packing Checklist, Figure 5.2.

MATERIALS PREPARATION CHECKLIST				

ITEM DATE				
1. FLIPCHART				
2. FLIPCHART MARKERS				
3. POINTER				
4. EMPLOYEE HANDOUTS				
5. PREPARATION FORM				
6. OHTs				
7. OHP PENS				
8. SLIDES				
9. VIDEOS/FILMS				
10. NOTEPAPER				
11. PENCILS				
12. MASKING TAPE				
13.				
14.				

Figure 5.2

The two blank rows at the bottom of the checklist are for any additional items you might want to add.

3. Prepare training area and equipment.
Before your session starts you should set up the room. An important factor here is the arrangement of tables and chairs. The way you arrange the furniture communicates a message and

99

The Staff Development Handbook

tells employees what kind of training session this will be. Your furniture arrangement depends on:

- the number of people in the session;
- the different types of training activities; and
- how much control you want over the session.

The diagrams in Figure 5.3 indicate the most common seating

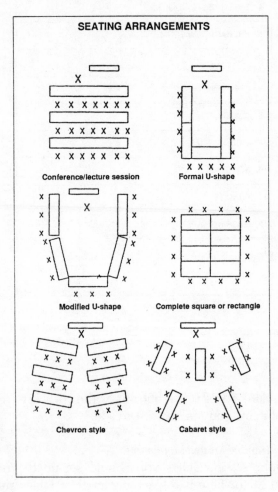

Figure 5.3

arrangements. Rows of tables and chairs indicate a *formal conference or lecture session* where large numbers of employees need to be accommodated and not much audience participation is expected. This arrangement provides a high degree of control but there is a lack of opportunity for employees to interact. If you want some participation in this setting, you need to encourage and provide opportunities for it, for example, by providing a question and answer session and encouraging people from the back to contribute.

The rather formal *U-shape* or more informal *modified U* are mainly used for training sessions which involve a presentation or demonstration supported by visual aids. The U-shape allows you to walk into and move about the U to increase your contact with employees and encourage involvement in discussion or practice. Employees at the rear of the U may, however, be far from the screen, flipchart or video. Small group work may also be difficult to set up, and you may need to move the furniture to provide the necessary separation of groups.

Furniture set out in a *cabaret* or *chevron style* indicates an emphasis on group work and not much formal presentation. These styles encourage an informal atmosphere and an exchange of ideas, where you can circulate freely. If you have to make a formal presentation, however, these arrangements may lead to a lack of attention among some people and side conversations may develop.

Another important preparation decision is how you will divide employees for any pair or group work. In particular, you may want to mix people and avoid putting employees from the same unit together. One of the things people look forward to when they attend a training session is to get a break from the same old faces, views and problems. Working with people from their own unit can therefore detract from employees' enjoyment and the productivity of the group. It may also lead to conflict and disruption when feelings which are suppressed on the job are set free in the 'safe setting' which a training session can provide.

Another point to consider here is whether you want employees to choose where they sit or not. Communication and the effectiveness of the training may be adversely affected if, at the beginning, employees only sit with the people they know. One way to ensure a 'mix' from the start is to write out employee name cards in advance and place them on the tables before people arrive. Not only do you and the employees benefit from the 'mix', but you avoid a 'cliquish' atmosphere at the beginning and the dangers of a small group injecting negative feelings about their jobs into the training.

As well as considering where employees will sit, consider your own position at the beginning of the session. Will you stand behind a podium; sit in a chair with no barrier between you and participants; stand at the front and move around a little? Will you first take one position and then shift to another? Your answers to these questions depend on the atmosphere you want to create; the nature of the opening activity; and what makes you feel comfortable. Using a podium provides a degree of formality and emphasizes your authority. The podium is appropriate for formal presentations and occasions like the opening of a conference or the beginning of an induction course for new staff. On the other hand, sitting in a chair with no barrier between you and participants indicates an informal relaxed approach with much discussion. If you choose to stand at the front and move around, the atmosphere is less relaxed and more purposeful; in particular, by moving towards employees you encourage their contributions and involvement. Quite often you will need to take up one position in order to make any introductory remarks, then shift to another position for the opening activity.

Most important of all, you should set up and check the equipment you will use. Make sure the overhead projector is ready, the video has been rewound and is ready to start at the beginning and there won't be any technical hitches to disrupt your session. Check the lighting and whether you can adjust it, eg for showing a video. You should also check the ventilation – a room that is stuffy or very warm may lull employees to sleep, especially if you need to talk for much of the time.

Finally, you should go to the back of the room and look at the visual arrangement from the employees' perspective. Is there anything distracting? Will everyone be able to see you, the flipchart or the overhead projector screen? Is this setting as business-like or attractive as you can make it?

By the time the employees arrive, you should be comfortably established in the training room and in control of the environment. If the room is prepared – the furniture arranged, equipment checked, paper, pens, name cards set out – employees will feel themselves entering a purposeful and professional training session. They will be more interested in the training and confident of its usefulness. The fact that everything is prepared and the possibility of mishaps has been virtually eliminated, will certainly make you feel more confident. You will be ready to play the gracious host or hostess and conduct a successful session.

4. Harness your nervous energy.
Even when all the preparations have been made, most people, especially those who are new to training, feel nervous before a training session. Successful trainers, however, control and harness this nervous energy, translating it into enthusiasm and activity. Below are some suggestions on how you might do this.

● Don't think about your anxieties but instead focus on your message and your audience. Think positively about the good things that will happen as a result of your training.

● When you arrive at the training site dissipate your nervous energy through physical action. Greet and talk to people, have tea or coffee with them and as much as possible make yourself feel at ease with the audience.

● Relieve any tension and anxiety by using deep breathing. When you are tense you hold your stomach rigid and breathe only in the upper chest; this only moves about a cupful of air. A full abdominal breath moves eight to ten times that amount – it supplies you with more oxygen, reduces fatigue and makes you more alert and ready to begin. To shift from chest to abdominal breathing, take a deep breath and then blow it out through your mouth like an audible sigh of relief.

● Avoid the risk of 'drying up' by having a cup of tea or coffee or a jug of water and a glass at the front of the room.

• When you are ready to begin, 'sweep' the room with your eyes and make eye contact with each person. From the employees' viewpoint, this conveys an air of command and confidence and makes them feel you are speaking personally to them.

• Many speakers, usually because they are nervous, start speaking too quickly. People begin to feel left behind and anxious – this is conveyed through their expressions, and the speaker becomes even more nervous. When you are ready to start, take a deep breath and begin strongly. Speak in a clear deliberate way and don't be afraid to pause, especially after your opening statement: audiences see such pauses as a sign of confidence and mastery.

• Avoid at all costs beginning in an apologetic tone. If you show a lack of confidence in conducting the training or giving the presentation, then you lose credibility.

• Avoid 'closed' or tense body positions and 'open up' through the use of gestures, facial expressions and a variety of tone and pitch. Move around a little and use gestures to dissipate any excess nervous energy. If you move towards employees this will help to develop rapport and involvement.

Conduct the session

The suggestions given below follow the guidelines in Figure 5.1. They also reflect the sequence presented in the training feedback form, Figure 4.5.

1. State session objective(s).
Lots of people think of beginning their training session with a joke. But only a few people are good tellers of jokes. Unless you really are effective at pacing, delivery and style, don't try telling jokes in formal situations.

If you want a stimulating opening, however, you might use an 'icebreaker question'. For example, 'Has anyone here had problems with this?', or 'What do you expect or want to learn from this session?' Questions like these encourage early involvement, stimulate interest and let you know at the beginning how people feel about the topic and your training.

Whether or not you use a joke or some other 'icebreaker', make sure your audience know the purpose of your session and what you're talking about from the start. If employees are going to be tested, tell them and state the specific performance objectives of your training session together with any conditions and standards of performance required. Emphasize that the objective(s) describes what the employee should be able to do by the end of your training session, not what you will do. Reinforce this statement of objective(s) by using a visual aid.

2. Relate objective(s) to employee jobs and interests.
Let employees know *what's in it for them* – what benefits they can gain from the training session. If employees know *how* the information or skill will help them in their jobs, how important it is or how frequently it arises, they are much more likely to want to learn.

If possible, relate your training session to off-the-job as well as on-the-job benefits.

3. Elicit employees' previous knowledge and experience.
A major obstacle to managers, supervisors or other experienced employees giving effective training is the fact that they tend to know too much. They have forgotten how difficult it was to learn something or how long it has taken them to become proficient in this area. They tend to assume too much, go quickly through new material and say things like, 'You should know this'.

It is most important, therefore, for you to know where employees are at the beginning and start at their level. Ask questions to find out what they already know or what previous experience they have had related to the session topic. You may find out that your employees already know quite a lot and this will save you repeating what they know. You may also find some 'experts' in the audience and be able to use them as a resource in any discussion activities. In this way you can save time and avoid people feeling bored or perhaps insulted by the level of material.

By asking questions early in the training session you can get employees involved and interested.

4. *Present main points of session.*

Books on how to make presentations often advise, 'Tell them what you're going to say, say it, then tell them what you've said'. In terms of sequence, therefore, you should provide an overview to emphasize the main points of the presentation and their relationship with each other. After presenting the 'big picture' you can provide the details necessary for understanding or implementing each of the main points. Here you should focus on those details that employees will *need to know*. The inclusion of *nice to know* details depends on the time available and what employees want to know. If they want more information, they might get this through the question and answer session, the discussion at the end of the presentation or through back-up reference materials. Finally, you should review the main points of the presentation again and lead into the question and answer or discussion session.

Inexperienced trainers tend to focus on the content of a presentation, making sure that nothing is omitted and every little detail included. Either through enthusiasm, a wish to show off expertise or a mistaken fear of 'short changing' employees, they are often tempted to stray from the objective, add 'nice to know' information and over-elaborate. The methods used in the presentation tend to be treated as an afterthought and employees stay silent, confused and suffering from 'information overload'.

The experienced trainer, however, focuses on content and methods together and breaks up the presentation into meaningful segments. Following the KISS principle (Keep It Short and Simple, or more colloquially, Keep It Simple Stupid) he or she makes everything as logical and as clear as possible. Rather than reading aloud from a textbook or from notes, the experienced trainer uses the preparation form and visual aids as cues. He or she tries to keep participants mentally and physically active by avoiding long stretches of 'trainer talk' and breaking up the presentation with questions, discussions and other activities.

5. Use visual aids to highlight main points.
For step-by-step guidelines on how to use visual aids, turn to the Appendix at the back of this book. The guidelines there deal with:

- handouts;
- flipcharts;
- overhead transparencies;
- slides;
- video.

6. Use questions to involve employees and check understanding.
During a training session it's important to ask questions to check how well employees understand. The use of questions has advantages in getting employees involved and interested and provides you with immediate feedback on the effectiveness of the training session. As you conduct your session, 'read' the audience. Blank or puzzled faces tell you to check on what people have learned, to give a practice or application activity or to start asking questions. Obviously you shouldn't move on to another point until you are sure the previous material has been understood.

Your use of questioning depends on the audience and the degree of involvement you need. For example you might use:

- rhetorical questions – questions you raise and answer yourself – when you want to enliven your presentation and make employees think;
- overhead questions – questions addressed to everyone – when you want to engage their attention. Then you might direct the question to a particular employee;
- direct questions – questions addressed to specific employees – when you want to quicken the pace and make some employees more attentive.

7. Encourage employee questions and comments.
By encouraging employees to ask questions and make comments you again increase their involvement and check their understanding. Make sure you provide some breaks in your presenta-

tion for questions to be asked, or allow a reasonable length of time at the end for a question and answer session. There are some suggestions for handling the question and answer period in the 'Common Situations' at the end of this chapter.

Whatever you do, don't force employees to leave all their questions until the last minute and then ask, 'Are there any questions?' At that point employees know the session is about to finish. They begin to 'tune out' and think about other things, while those who really want to ask questions will not do so for fear of taking up the others' time.

8. Use appropriate delivery skills.

● *Interest and enthusiasm* are infectious. Show interest and enthusiasm in your topic and in what employees have to contribute when they ask questions or make points. Smile, especially if you feel tense, and this will make you and your audience feel more relaxed.

● *Eye contact* should be established with employees particularly at the beginning of the session. Avoid talking to the flipchart or overhead projector.

● *Gestures and movement* should be natural and use your nervous energy. Rather than being locked into rigid positions or pacing from side to side, you should be fluid. Move naturally towards the audience when you ask questions or want more involvement. Avoid hiding your hands in your pockets and use natural hand gestures to emphasize key points or generate enthusiasm.

● *Voice.* Speak loudly enough for everyone in the room to hear. Don't speak too quickly and vary your pace of speech and tone to emphasize key points. Don't be afraid to pause and speak deliberately when you are starting to explain a new phase or step in the training session.

● *Language.* Make sure your language is understandable and you avoid jargon or slang. Choose words and ideas that are in the employees' vocabulary and use simple explanations and examples if you are presenting a difficult idea or concept.

9. Provide enough time to apply/practise new information.
Time for application and practice is particularly important in job training. In a training session on how to use some new equipment, procedures or techniques, some demonstration and employee practice are required (For more information on demonstration and practice, see Chapter 3.) In order to conduct practice effectively, you need to:

- Provide a constructive and relaxed environment – an atmosphere of 'all colleagues together' and of people helping each other to improve. Give encouragement and private feedback on the employee practice.
- Give employees more than one chance. If they know that they have several opportunities to practise or demonstrate a skill, they tend to feel more relaxed. They can make mistakes and learn from them.

10. Evaluate/review the session.
Every training session, like every presentation, should have a beginning, a middle and an end. The middle of a session is usually full of information and activities and when employees get really involved in discussion or practice there is a tendency to let things 'run on'. The result is there is not much time for evaluation or a review of what's been accomplished. Both you and the employees may finish the training feeling that things were not fully completed or the training was not 'rounded off'.

At the end of a training session, therefore, make sure there is some time for a concluding activity that will bring together and apply the knowledge or skills learned in the session. The concluding activity is useful in the following ways.

- It provides some feedback or evaluation of employee learning. For example, if you conducted a pre-test before the training session, then it's natural to give a post-test at the end.
- It can lead to an evaluation and discussion of the performances

or the products that are a result of the session. For example, you might discuss the reports produced by the groups who have worked on a particular task or problem.

- It reviews what's been accomplished and links training to the job. Employees tend to 'turn off' and think about going home when they hear phrases like 'Now let's review what we've done', 'Now I'm going to summarize'. It's more effective to focus on the present or the future with comments like 'Let's pick out the key points we can use', or 'Write down three things that you've learned and that you are going to use in your job'. With this kind of review you can maintain employee involvement – even more vital here because you are looking for commitment and transfer to the job.

Common situations

Situation: You don't think you'll be able to remember everything you need to say. You want to read your speech.
Response: If you read your speech, you are ensuring a monotonous and boring training session or presentation. Use notes, handouts, flipchart pages and overhead transparencies to provide your outline and key points as you speak. When you use visual aids in this way as cues, your mind can select words spontaneously. Your voice is naturally more active and interesting because you are continuously thinking and adapting your presentation to the audience.

Situation: You begin to speak but suddenly feel yourself 'drying up'. Your voice starts to quiver and you come to a halt.
Response: Try to relax. Pause and have a sip of water. Take a deep breath and look at a friendly face in the audience. Then start to speak again. Try to smile – this will help you relax and generally connect better with the audience. The audience indeed may not notice the brief interruption – what seems like eternity to you is in reality often only a few seconds. They may take your hesitation as simply a natural pause in the flow of the presentation.

Situation: You have just started your training session. Every time you try to make a point, the door opens and more people come into the room.

Response: To prevent this situation arising, make sure everyone knows the correct starting time and how to get to the training room. Then make sure the front seats are filled and leave some empty ones near the door so that latecomers can slip in without disturbing the others.

If this situation does arise, however, and people walk in, carry on with your session. By constantly stopping and starting you will disrupt the training and penalize those people who did arrive on time.

No matter how annoyed you feel, don't lock the door. When employees knock on a door to get in they not only disrupt the training session but give a bad impression of training as a whole.

Situation: As you are making your presentation, an employee interrupts to ask a question. The annoying thing is that the question relates to a point you are about to come to. If this person waited a few moments, he or she would receive the answer to the question.

Response: This interruption may be a danger sign indicating that your presentation is too long or that too many questions are being left unanswered. It may be time for you to stop, answer the employee's question and ask if anyone else has questions at this point. If your presentation is not long, however, stop, smile and tell the employee that you are just about to come to that point. If he or she waits, you hope to deal with most questions. There will also be time at the end of the presentation and you will be pleased to answer questions then.

Situation: You are leading a discussion and one employee who has hardly spoken so far disagrees strongly with an important point that you make. The employee seems emotional about the issue.

Response: Treat the employee's disagreement as a positive and welcome contribution to the discussion. Make eye contact, smile and use encouraging phrases like 'I see', 'Ah-ah', or 'Can you tell us more about that?' Ask the employee to clarify or add to what he or she has said and use additional questions to assess the level of disagreement. Quite often the disagreement will be the result of a misunderstanding or based on a difference of emphasis. Sometimes the outburst may be the result of work frustrations or a desire for attention. If the disagreement relates to critical points in the training material however, this needs to be discussed openly. You should try to find out if other employees have similar views but are not expressing them.

If you finally disagree with the employee's idea or comment make it clear that you are rejecting the viewpoint not the participant. Try to involve the person even more in discussion and the training activities.

Avoid treating differences as obstacles, as expressions of negative attitudes, or as personal attacks. Instead treat differences constructively, as opportunities to discuss different views and as contributing to the success of training. If you treat differences positively, this adds to the variety and interest of the course. Employees become more involved and as a result can learn more.

Situation: During a discussion two employees have contradictory views and start to argue with each other.
Response: Don't take sides in the argument. Point out the usefulness of any points the employees make and, if the discussion is relevant to your objectives and information, invite other employees to contribute. If the issues raised by the two employees are not particularly relevant however, thank them for expressing their views and move on.

Situation: During the question and answer session, an employee makes some 'hostile' comments and asks a question which seems to attack the organization, you personally or your topic.
Response: Try if possible to agree with at least one aspect of the questioner's comments. Never be discourteous to the questioner – if you are, employees will tend to support him or her. Try to understand what the person is saying and their feelings. Ask him or her to clarify points or give further details or examples to ensure that you understand. If necessary, rephrase and divide the question up into parts. Then answer each part in turn.

Situation: During the question and answer session, an employee starts to give a speech expressing his or her opinions.

Response: Don't lose your temper or show any anger. Ask the employee to state his or her question so that you can respond. If the employee continues to make a speech, emphasize the purpose of the question and answer session and say that you will be pleased to discuss these concerns with the employee after the training session. Ask for the next question.

Situation: You are involved in your training session and get carried away with your subject. You notice that you have only 10 minutes left, but you have more than 10 minutes' material left to present. Cutting the training session short will mean you miss out important material and make the session look unprofessional.

Response: To prevent this situation arising, rehearse your training session and leave enough time for discussion, questions and answers and any practice required.

If this situation does arise however, cover the remaining key points and attempt to deal with the details during the question and answer or skill-practice sessions.

Situation: In the question and answer session you face the following:

1. *Someone asks a question that is beyond your ability to handle.*
2. *Someone keeps asking follow-up questions to the original one.*
3. *The time is over, but some people have not had their questions answered.*

Responses:

1. Suggest that you and the questioner do some research and discuss the question at a later date.
2. If other people are wanting to ask questions, point this out and move on to the next questioner. If there is a lack of participation, try to broaden the discussion by asking other employees to comment on or respond to the person's follow-up questions.
3. Try to respond to the questions privately after the training session.

Action items

Evaluate the effectiveness of your training session by asking yourself and responding to the following questions:

1. What went well?

2. What problems arose in the training session?

3. How could the session be improved?

4. How can I improve?

5. Are employees using the training on the job?

6. Are they experiencing any problems?

7. Is any further training needed?

CHAPTER 6

How to Improve Performance Through Off-the-job Training

'In the last analysis the individual must develop himself, and he will do so optimally only in terms of what he sees as meaningful and valuable. If he becomes an active party in the decisions that are made about his development, he is likely to make the most of the opportunities that are presented'. Douglas McGregor, *The Human Side of Enterprise.*

In all the discussion about manpower planning, training and productivity the individual can sometimes be forgotten. But as Douglas McGregor emphasized over 30 years ago, in the end the individual must choose to develop him or herself. Training and development can only be effective if employees want to change what they do. This is perhaps even more true of off-the-job training which deals with developing interpersonal, supervisory and management skills than it is of on-the-job training which generally focuses on technical skill development.

The aim of this chapter is to help you select appropriate off-the-job training courses for your employees and to involve them in ensuring there is a 'transfer of learning' – that what they learn on the course improves their job performance.

Your current situation

1. What off-the-job courses have you attended in the past?

2. Why did you attend?

3. What did you learn?

4. What information or skills from the course(s) have you used on the job?

Consider your responses to these questions in the light of the following comments:

Your responses
1. If you have not attended any courses, you need to look at your own personal and professional development. Consider the importance and benefits of off-the-job training described later in this chapter.

2. If you can't identify the reasons, then your boss didn't brief you or it was ineffectively done. What important reasons might there be for sending some of your staff on off-the-job courses? This chapter will help you to identify some possible staff training needs.

3. If you can't list some specific things you learned, then the training was not very effective. Look at the Guidelines given in this chapter for improving the effectiveness of off-the-job training.

4. If you couldn't or didn't use the information or skills you learned, again the training wasn't very effective. What would have made it easier for you to apply what you learned? If your boss had been more involved, would that have helped? The transfer of 'learning' to job situations is a critical issue in the effectiveness of off-the-job training courses. This chapter gives some guidelines and suggestions on how you can ensure this 'learning transfer'.

Why off-the-job training and education is important

The message of this book is that there is a lot more to staff development than sending people on training courses. However, off-the-job training courses are important because they can provide the following.

● Opportunities for staff to maintain and increase their technical or professional expertise. Organizations recruit people for their specific skills and experience but if employees' skills and expertise are not maintained and updated, their value decreases.

● Types of training and expertise that are not available in the workplace. Professional trainers have access to expertise, training materials, equipment and facilities that will help your staff to learn new information and skills.

● Opportunities for constructive thinking and planning. A period away from the pressures of the job can give your staff the time and space they need for creative thinking and planning. They can gain a broader perspective on their job and role in the organization.

Whether the absence from work is for a day or several weeks, the greatest problem with off-the-job training is whether employees can transfer what they learned on the course to what happens on the job afterwards. Off-the-job training can only be effective if employees return to a work environment that supports change and individual growth. A negative environment will make them reluctant to attend off-the-job courses or make them feel this training is a waste of time. Common responses in training courses are: 'My boss should be here instead of me' and 'This is all theoretical – it won't work in our department'. A negative environment where people do things as they've always done them can quickly erase any learning.

Your role is crucial here. If you and your staff are going to get the results you want from the experience and investment in off-the-job training, you need to integrate it and use the training as a stimulus and support for growth on the job.

The extra attention you need to give to ensure that off-the-job training leads to improved work performance is small, however, compared to the costs of course fees, travel and lost production time.

Benefits of off-the-job training

What's in it for you
Off-the-job training courses have the following advantages.

- They give your staff an 'outside perspective' so that they know what's happening in the world beyond your organization. They can learn how other people are doing the job and can bring back into your department some new ideas and suggestions for improvements.

- They provide an opportunity for your staff to meet with people from other departments or companies and share ideas and information. In particular, the kind of 'networking' which goes on at training courses can lubricate the operation when your people get back to the job. The people they met on the course can often help them find a way through organizational red tape and bureaucracy.

- They improve your people's versatility and make them better equipped to deal with new tasks, projects and responsibilities. In particular, off-the-job training courses can prepare staff for promotion and new roles in the department. Attendance at a supervisory skills course will increase an employee's knowledge and skills in supervision and bring him or her into contact with other new and potential supervisors. Your employee will be able to discuss common supervisory problems and pick up new ideas.

- They refresh your people. Employees usually enjoy the change of scene and people. If the course is relevant and you follow-up with the person, it can provide him or her with a new lease of life.

What's in it for the employee

Off-the-job training courses can make employees feel the following.

- 'At last somebody's noticed me'. When you send an employee on a course, this shows that you are paying attention to him or her – and attention is probably the greatest motivator of all.

- 'Now I can see the big picture'. Off-the-job training often provides an overview of the topic so that employees can put their own job and experience into a broader context. Distance may not lend enchantment but can enable employees to get a mental grip on their situation and see that other people have similar problems and concerns.

- 'I'm keeping up with my profession – improving my future prospects'. There is nothing worse than feeling you are in a 'dead-end job' with little opportunity for change or improvement. Off-the-job training courses enable employees to maintain and update their professional expertise. This is not just a matter of maintaining 'certification' or meeting professional or government requirements. The positive effect on employees' morale and professional self-confidence, their sense that the organization is promoting their growth, is even more important.

- 'Now I can concentrate'. Off-the-job training courses provide a controlled environment in which employees can concentrate on learning new information or skills. There are no job interruptions or distractions and employees are away from the emotional atmosphere of the workplace. This distance is particularly helpful where changes in attitudes are required or employees need to improve and practice interpersonal skills.

- 'Nobody's trying to catch me out'. When training is off-the-job employees have the freedom to practise in a non-threatening environment. An employee's failure or lack of success isn't going to be noticed or recorded by colleagues.

● 'I'd like to try that'. Off-the-job courses often provide new ideas and perspectives for improving employee's individual work – new ideas that might be used for improving the job and the operation of the department.

Off-the-job training guidelines

The guidelines in Figure 6.1 outline how you can make off-the-job training courses more effective in improving your employees' performance and the operations of your department. The notes below explain and give suggestions on how you might use the guidelines.

Preparation

1. Identify the need for training and development.
The specific need might be organizational. For example, changes in departmental workload and direction might require employees to gain additional knowledge and skills. Technological change may require you to send staff on computer courses or the departure of qualified staff may require you to enrol people for health and safety training.

Alternatively, the specific need might be individual. A performance review might highlight an employee's need for further training and development or you might need to prepare someone for promotion or new responsibilities.

2. Decide on the appropriate method.
Given a specific organizational or individual need, you should decide what might be the best response or combination of responses. Would on-the-job training, mentored work experience, delegation, open learning or an off-the-job training course be most appropriate? In some situations one response is clearly suitable; however, in many situations a combination of responses is best. For example, if you wanted a newly promoted supervisor to learn about your organization's performance review system you might use the following training pattern:

OFF-THE-JOB TRAINING GUIDELINES

PREPARATION

1. IDENTIFY NEED FOR TRAINING OR DEVELOPMENT ☐

2. DECIDE APPROPRIATE METHOD ☐

3. SELECT APPROPRIATE OFF-THE-JOB TRAINING COURSE ☐

4. BRIEF EMPLOYEE ON COURSE ☐

5. ASSIGN REPLACEMENT WHILE EMPLOYEE IS ABSENT ☐

FOLLOW-UP

1. DISCUSS COURSE WITH EMPLOYEE ☐

2. DISCUSS AND AGREE ON ACTION PLAN ☐

3. UPDATE EMPLOYEE'S FILE ☐

4. ASSESS VALUE OF COURSE ☐

5. DECIDE IF FURTHER TRAINING IS NECESSARY ☐

Figure 6.1

- The supervisor attends an off-the-job course on how to conduct performance reviews. The course provides an introduction to the principles and methods used in performance review.
- You or your representative hold a discussion/coaching session with the supervisor. This session involves a review of the course material and a discussion of how this applies to your organization's performance review policies and procedures.
- The supervisor watches a video or reads some articles or a handbook on performance review (see Chapter 10 of this book).
- He or she works on some performance review forms with you or your representative serving as a mentor.
- The supervisor rehearses some performance review sessions based upon the completed forms. You or your representative play the part of the employees in these performance review discussions.

In this example the training pattern combines off-the-job training with follow-up on the job.

3. Select an appropriate training course.
The Course Selection Checklist, Figure 6.2, will help you find out whether a particular course fits your staff's training and development needs. Notes on each item in the checklist are given below.

The company offering this course is known and has a good reputation.
This doesn't mean you should dismiss reputable new companies, but it's easier to gather information about older ones. Do you know anyone or any other organization that has used this company or training course? If you do, check whether they would use them again.

The course seems to fit the jobs and experience levels of my people.
What kinds of employees are expected to enrol for this course? Does the course literature specify types of job, levels of expe-

COURSE SELECTION CHECKLIST

COURSE REQUIREMENTS	YES	NO
1. The company offering this course is known and has a good reputation		
2. The course seems to fit the jobs and experience level of my people ⸙		
3. Employees need to prepare for the course		
4. The course has specfic learning objectives that are relevant to my people and their jobs ⸙		
5. The course content is described and is relevant to my people and their jobs ⸙		
6. There seems to be enough time to deal with the course content and achieve these objectives ⸙		
7. The methods used in the course seem to be participative and action oriented ⸙		
8. Modern training aids e.g. computers, video, are used in the course		
9. The course leaders seem well-qualified with the kind of experience that will help my people ⸙		
10. The course leaders provide some follow-up after the course		
Considering all of the above factors the investment in training is justified		

Indicates key items ⸙

Figure 6.2

rience or particular backgrounds? Do the people you want to attend fit the description?

Employees need to prepare for the course.
Preparation assignments indicate that the people conducting the course are concerned about transfer of learning to the workplace. Preparation may involve employees being required to discuss the course objectives and their own individual objectives with their manager or supervisor. Preparation may also involve employees conducting research on their own organization as the basis for a work-based project.

The course has specific learning objectives that are relevant to my people and their jobs.
Does the course literature identify specific learning objectives or are there only vague 'aims' or 'outcomes' mentioned? If there are no specific learning objectives, it will be difficult to measure the effectiveness of the course.

The course content is described and is relevant to my people and their jobs.
Does the course literature provide an outline of the topics and the content dealt with in the course? Is this course content relevant to your people and their jobs?

There seems to be enough time to deal with the course content and achieve these objectives.
Beware of picking a course because it's short and cheap. Ask yourself: Do the objectives seem reasonable and realistic given the course duration? Is there enough time to deal with this course content? Learning is not a fast business, particularly when you want your people to acquire skills. Employees need time to assimilate new information, to discuss, practise, apply and troubleshoot: they need time to learn. There's not much point in sending your people to a cheap course where they don't learn.

The methods used in the course seem to be participative and action-oriented.
Does the course information include an agenda with time allotted for employees to raise questions, discuss issues and think about

how they might apply what they have learned back on the job? Will employees be involved in a variety of activities or will they mainly sit and listen? Action planning is often a feature of good courses. Check with the course literature or the course leaders whether there are opportunities for action planning and the transfer of learning back to the job.

Modern training aids, eg, computers, video, are used in the course.
Training aids don't guarantee learning, but the use of these aids does show that the course leaders appreciate that technology is part of the business environment and can increase learning.

The course leaders seem well-qualified with the kind of experience that will help my people.
What are the course leaders' qualifications and experience – business, government service, or academic only? Have they published books or articles on topics to be dealt with in the course?

The course leaders provide some follow-up after the course.
Follow-up sessions or visits to the work site show that the training staff are serious about the 'transfer of learning' and improved performance at the workplace. Follow-up also gives you an opportunity to meet the course leaders, to learn more about the course and what your people are learning.

If you can answer 'Yes' to the key statements, then the investment in off-the-job training is justified. If you can't, then you should look at other courses.

4. *Brief the employee on the course and why he or she is being sent.*
This briefing is important for three main reasons:

- Employees often arrive at training courses with little or no idea of why they are there. They are not mentally prepared and this reduces the effectiveness of the training.
- Some employees think they are being criticized if their manager sends them on a training course. This makes them

resistant to learning and creates problems during and after the course. When you brief such an employee, you should explain that the training is not a punishment but an opportunity. Your own attitude to training and development and your tone are critical here.

- If there is no briefing, the employee may think the training is unimportant, and may not be ready to apply his or her learning to the job. He or she may see the course as a holiday break.

At the briefing, discuss your reasons for sending the employee on the course. Discuss what you hope he or she will get out of the training, and what will be expected of him or her on their return. Discuss any preparation that may need to be done and any concerns that the employee may have. Those who are limited in their experience of training might be anxious that they may not be successful, have a dread of showing their limitations or retain unhappy memories of school. They may need more explanation and some reassurance that the training is not a test. Those who are used to being trained and attending courses are likely to be more confident and need less explanation.

The material in most off-the-job courses is generalized in an attempt to be appropriate to all. During the discussion you and the employee might identify skills that he or she will concentrate on developing during and after the course. Help your employee select a specific job situation, task or problem to which each skill can be applied. This discussion will help your employee to tailor the material to his or her own needs and develop a post-course action plan.

Finally, only send people to courses who want to go. People can't be forced to learn but they can prevent other people from learning. Don't expect training courses to change personalities.

5. *Assign a replacement while the employee is absent.*
If the employee is going to be away for more than a few days, assign someone else to deal with the workload. Try also to avoid disturbing the employee while he or she is on the course. Constant telephone calls about work problems will disrupt the employee's involvement in the training and hinder learning.

These interruptions will also alienate him or her and give the lie to your statements about staff development.

You should also avoid piling up work for the employee's return. We all know of managers or supervisors who welcome their employees back from training courses with a gloating 'Now you're back in the real world' attitude. They point to all the work piled up on the desk or gleefully tell the employee about all the problems that have arisen during their absence and what they now have to deal with.

Follow-Up

1. Discuss the course with the employee.
As soon as possible after the completion of the course let your people tell you what they have done and how they think they can use what they have learned. You might use an evaluation form like the Training Course Evaluation, Figure 6.3, as a basis for this discussion.

2. Discuss and agree on an action plan.
Discuss with the employee what might happen as a result of the course. An action plan might involve the employee:

- Giving a briefing or report on the course for the benefit of others in the department.
- Making plans to use the new knowledge or practise the skills on the job. Somone who has just attended a computer skills course might use the computer to work on his or her next project.
- Training someone in the department in a skill he or she has learned from the course.

3. Update the training and development section of the employee file.
Change can be overlooked either because we are too distant from people or too close to them to recognize their growth. We tend to have a fixed image in our minds as to what Grace or Christopher are like and what they are capable of – she's a satisfactory employee, etc – and we often don't take the time to stand back,

---

TRAINING COURSE EVALUATION

Course Title:_____

Date:_____ Location:_____

Course Leader(s):_____

Please evaluate the course in the following areas by checking the appropriate rating: **E** for Excellent
VG for Very Good
G for Good
F for Fair
P for Poor

STATEMENT	E	VG	G	F	P
1. Course relevance and usefulness in job					
2. Participation and involvement					
3. Practical discussion and exercises					
4. Sufficient time for course activities					
5. Overall effectiveness of course leader (s)					
6. Overall effectiveness of course					
7.					
8.					

Write in the spaces above other statements you want feedback on.

Figure 6.3

TRAINING COURSE EVALUATION

Identify three things you learned from the course:

1._____

_____

2._____

_____

3._____

_____

Explain how you will apply these three things on the job:

1._____

_____

2._____

_____

3._____

_____

Was this course at the right time in your job and career?

_____

_____

_____

Additional comments / suggestion: _____

_____

_____

_____

_____

Employee signature:_____

Figure 6.3 *(cont)*

review and adjust it. People can be completely turned off work when they realize their development has not been registered and they are being held down as a result.

Individual training and development plans provide a record of courses and planned development activities. See the 'Action Items' section for an example of a plan. Such plans help you to build up a picture of someone's growth. A joint discussion on this updating can both jog your memory and let people know that you are up-to-date on their progress. Maintaining records of achievement and progress helps you to keep your view of staff up-to-date and provides information for performance review.

4. Assess the value of the course to the individual and to the department.
You need to consider both the immediate and long-term value of the course. The immediate value of technical and skills training courses can be observed on the job but it is not so easy to judge the value of courses which involve the development of interpersonal skills.

You shouldn't ignore long-term development, however. Employees can improve by small increments and almost imperceptibly in terms of their value to your operation. And in the end there is a massive difference between supervising a bunch of experienced people who have developed in terms of their knowledge and skills and those who have not. There are enormous differences in productivity between one group of middle-aged staff who are motivated, producing more and looking for more challenge and responsibility and another group who have plateaued and are going through the motions, serving their time until retirement.

5. Decide whether further training or experience is necessary.
Sometimes a training programme may be modular and in order to gain the required skills the employee may need to attend further courses. If so, you need to plan for and schedule future attendance. Sometimes you may judge that the individual and your operation would benefit from the employee gaining additional training or experience. For example, one of your employees might have attended a 'train the trainer' course and shown

interest and some ability in this area. You might schedule him or her for more courses so that you have a specialist trainer in your department.

Common situations

Situation: When you brief the employee on the course he/she says they don't need the skill and don't want to go on the course.
Response: Look back to your preparation and why you decided there was a need for training and development. Make sure the employee fully understands the reasons why you are sending him or her on the course. If there is still resistance try to find out the reasons. If the employee considers this training as a slight upon his/her abilities, emphasize the 'refresher' and developmental aspects of the training. If the employee feels 'I know this already', discuss how the course might increase his or her knowledge and skills and how the 'learning' can be applied when the person returns. However, if the employee is still resistant to this training, ask him or her to reconsider and set a date for further discussion.

The employee's motivation – the need he or she feels for new knowledge or increased skill – is the critical factor if any learning is to take place. Don't send people to courses if they really don't want to go.

Situation: The employee says he or she didn't benefit from the course. Other employees, however, have reported favourably on the training.
Response: Ask the employee why he or she didn't benefit and try to identify specific reasons. Employees often don't criticize off-the-job training courses because they want to be sent on other courses or they enjoyed the break. You may find that the course may suit some employees but not others.

Situation: The employee has some new ideas and suggestions about changing things. You've been doing this job for a long time and don't think these new ideas or suggestions will work.
Response: In your discussion after the course, you need to listen to what your employee has to say. Avoid dismissing new ideas

too easily. You might discuss your own experience and give your reasons why you think something might not work. Be open to change, though, and try to see how some of the new ideas might be accommodated. Something might be tried out for a trial period or the employee might 'pilot' it. Generally, when your employees return from training courses, try to encourage them to use their newly acquired knowledge and skills. If you don't, you and your department will be the losers.

Situation: One of your employees is involved in a long college-based or open learning course. After a good start the employee is making slow progress and seems to be losing interest in the course.

Reponse: Meet with the employee to discuss the course and show your interest in his or her progress. You may need to arrange regular discussions on progress because many employees need their manager or supervisor's interest and support to keep them going.

Situation: The employee is looking for some 'reward' for his or her attendance at a course and the extra effort involved. The employee thinks that because of attendance, he or she is due for promotion.

Response: In the pre-course discussion, you should have made the reasons for the employee going on the course clear. Refer back to these reasons if the employee raises the promotion issue. Point out that the organization is providing opportunities for technical and professional development and the 'reward' lies in the development of the employee's knowledge and skills. Explain that as far as promotion is concerned, this is dependent on a number of factors – the situation in the organization and department, the availability of positions, individual job performance over a period of time, seniority, etc. A person's training experience or qualifications are important factors when an employee is considered for promotion but not the only ones. He or she will now have to apply this recent training on the job and improve his or her work performance.

Situation: The employee fails the course.

Response: Discuss the situation with the employee and together identify the reasons for his or her failure. People don't all learn at the same pace and if you are satisfied that the employee has put in a reasonable effort, be sympathetic and support him or her in taking the course again.

Action items

Produce a Training and Development Record for each member of your staff. The form shown in Figure 6.4 might be useful to you both as a record of courses completed and of the courses you want the employee to take. First enter the names of the courses the person has attended, their duration, and the completion dates. Then enter the names of the courses you want the person to attend over the next year and schedule them if possible.

TRAINING AND DEVELOPMENT RECORD		
Employee Name:		
TRAINING AND DEVELOPMENT COURSES	DURATION	COMPLETION DATE

Figure 6.4

CHAPTER 7
How to Conduct Effective Team Meetings

Key Meeting Facts
The following statistics are extracted from a survey of 1000 American business leaders.

- Only 33% of the business leaders surveyed had formal training in how to run meetings.
- 75% of respondents said it was 'almost essential' to have a meeting agenda, but respondents indicated that they use agendas only 50% of the time.
- Almost 72% of business leaders surveyed currently spent more time in meetings than they did five years ago.
- More than 33% of the time spent in meetings was judged to be unproductive, costing businesses $37 billion.

Quoted in 'Making the most of meeting time', P.M. Tobia and M.C. Becker, in *Training and Development Journal*, August 1990.*

The statistics given above confirm what most people already know from bitter experience. Enormous amounts of time and money are wasted in disorganized business meetings. Generally, the blame for unproductive meetings tends to be directed towards the chairperson or leader of the meeting. He or she called the meeting for no clear purpose, was unprepared, didn't manage the meeting very well and failed to achieve anything. Effectiveness, however, also depends upon the preparation and techniques used by meeting participants.

	MEETINGS CHECKLIST	
	STATEMENT	
1	The meeting takes place in a constructive atmosphere rather than a critical or negative atmosphere.	
2	The meeting has clear purpose(s) or objective(s).	
3	An agenda is prepared and circulated prior to the meeting.	
4	Meeting participants have an opportunity to contribute items to the agenda.	
5	The 'right' people are invited to the meeting and there are no 'redundant' members.	
6	Meeting facilities are comfortable and adequate for the number of participants.	
7	The meeting begins on time.	
8	The meeting has a scheduled finishing time and finishes at that time.	
9	The meeting leader uses questions to stimulate discussion and periodically summarizes to move the meeting along.	
10	Participant contributions are welcome and everyone has an opportunity to present his or her point of view.	
11	Participants listen attentively and respond to one another.	
12	Someone 'takes the minutes' and at the end of each agenda topic the decisions and actions agreed on are reviewed.	
13	There is a focus on problem-solving and participants have a voice in decisions made at the meeting.	
14	Meeting participants show a willingness to compromise. There is little personal conflict and few arguments.	
15	When appropriate, visual aids are used to present information and are effective.	
16	If used, audio-visual equipment is in good working order.	
17	The focus is on team productivity and little time is wasted on personal or trivial items.	
18	The meeting usually ends with a summary of meeting accomplishments and action agreed upon.	
19	A memorandum or minutes of the meeting is circulated to each participant following the meeting.	
20	The meeting leader follows-up with participants on action agreed during the meeting.	

Figure 7.1

This chapter will help you to assess the effectiveness of the team meetings you conduct and attend. It will also suggest some steps for making them more productive in terms of improving staff performance and getting the job done.

Your current situation

Figure 7.1 contains a list of statements which apply to meetings. Check the statements that apply to the meetings you normally conduct. If the statement partially applies put a question mark (?). If the statement does not apply at all put an X.

All the statements in Figure 7.1 describe characteristics of effective meetings. Look at the statements against which you put either a ? or an X. What steps do you think you should take to make your meetings more effective?

Why effective team meetings are important

Making your meetings more effective is important because enormous amounts of time and money are wasted in business meetings. In large organizations, managers and supervisors can spend between 60 and 75 per cent of their working day either preparing for meetings, attending meetings or following up on meetings. In 1989 *Fortune* magazine spent a day shadowing Chrysler's chief operating officer, Robert Lutz, and found that for almost 10 hours out of an 11.5 hour day Lutz was involved in meetings. Less dramatically a survey of 160 British managers showed that executives spent about half their time in formal or informal meetings.

Not surprisingly, many managers feel prisoners of a meeting schedule that leaves little time for individual thought or achievement. Indeed, the situation seems to be worsening with the number of meetings increasing – a symptom of the ineffectiveness of the meetings already held.

Reasons for ineffective meetings
There are many reasons why meetings can be ineffective; a list of the most common follows.

● *There are no clear objectives and meetings seem unnecessary.*
Meetings take place because 'We always have a meeting on Monday', or 'It's time for the committee to get together'. Many of the people attending feel they could use the time more productively.

● *There is no agenda.*
Consequently, there is a lack of direction with meeting participants not clear about the purposes of meetings, the decisions made or responsibilities. The lack of an agenda and a finishing time leads to meetings going on forever and a lot of time being wasted on trivialities.

● *Communication is one-way.*
Meetings consist of the leader making a series of announcements with some time allowed for questions at the end. A circular or memo seems more appropriate than a costly meeting which people feel is a waste of their valuable time.

● *Participants are generally reluctant to speak.*
This may be due to individual embarrassment or a wish to get the meeting over with because it's wasting time. This reluctance, however, is sometimes due to participants' fear of negative reactions from the leader or the other participants. They want to stay out of trouble and therefore say nothing. If asked to report on their activities they say they have 'Nothing to report'.

● *Any new ideas that are proposed are destroyed or accepted without discussion.*
Again this happens when meetings take place in a negative atmosphere and people are reluctant to 'rock the boat'. The desire to conform and agree with the leadership destroys any new ideas which the leadership do not immediately agree with. When the leadership or influential participants put new proposals forward they are not adequately criticized or discussed.

● *Arguments and personal conflict undermine meeting productivity.*
Again this is often due to a negative, critical climate where people

score points off each other and try to accumulate credits with the meeting leader. Personal arguments take up the time that should be devoted to the task or problem in hand.

- *There is no action after meetings.*

The frequency of meetings means there is no time for action and meetings become a substitute for action. The comment, 'I haven't had time to do it. I'm just on my way to a meeting' is not uncommon. Lack of follow-up action also means that decisions are always subject to change and people argue over the same issues at successive meetings.

A simple answer to this problem would be to arbitrarily reduce the number of formal meetings in organizations. Meetings are important, however, because they can improve communication from and to management. They also help managers monitor the total operation and an effective meeting provides a snapshot of what's happening in a department. By promoting better communication within the organization, effective team meetings can improve the organization's health and employee morale.

Benefits of effective meetings

What's in it for you

Effective meetings can achieve the following.

- Improve team effectiveness and communication in your department. When work relationships only develop on a one-to-one basis, staff can feel isolated from each other. Sometimes a destructive competitiveness develops through a 'divide and rule approach' taken by some leaders. Balance the time you spend with individuals and that you spend with the group.

- Encourage people to review what they are doing and their progress towards meeting deadlines. If you have regular meetings people think more about their work because they want to contribute something worthwhile to the meeting when they get a chance.

• Improve the quality of your decision-making. Good decisions often depend on team members contributing what they know and a full and free discussion of the topic with a variety of views and perspectives expressed.

• Help to develop your staff. People can give mini-presentations and reports and respond to questions on their own assignments and special projects.

What's in it for meeting participants
Effective team meetings can lead to the following.

• Provide an overview of what's happening in the organization and the department and of what can affect people in future. Meetings can help bring employees who are new to your department 'up to speed quickly'. It is a good idea to have a meeting just after a new person has joined the department.

• Encourage team cooperation and team spirit. At effective meetings team members can stimulate each other and 'springboard' off each other's ideas.

• Provide employees with the opportunity to give feedback to the manager and to each other. Members learn more about and can be considerate of the manager and other participants' problems.

Guidelines for effective meetings

Guidelines for preparing and conducting effective meetings are shown in Figure 7.2. The notes below describe each of the steps in turn and provide suggestions on how to follow the guidelines.

Preparation

1. Identify the purpose or objective(s) of your meeting.
Avoid the trap of meeting through habit or too often. Ask yourself, 'Why is this meeting necessary?' If you can't think of a

---

EFFECTIVE MEETINGS - GUIDELINES

PREPARATION

1. IDENTIFY PURPOSE OR OBJECTIVE(S) OF MEETING ☐
2. IDENTIFY DECISIONS/ACTIONS YOU WANT TAKEN ☐
3. DEVELOP THE AGENDA ☐
4. SEND PARTICIPANTS COPIES OF AGENDA ☐
5. PREPARE YOUR OWN TOPICS/RESPONSIBILITIES ☐
6. CHECK VISUAL AIDS YOU PLAN TO USE ☐

TEN COMMANDMENTS FOR MANAGING MEETINGS

1. START MEETING ON TIME ☐
2. STATE MEETING OBJECTIVE(S) CLEARLY ☐
3. KEEP RECORDS OF MEETING ☐
4. ENSURE ADEQUATE DISCUSSION OF TOPICS ☐
5. PUSH TOWARDS DECISIONS AND ACTIONS ☐
6. MANAGE THE USE OF TIME ☐
7. MANAGE CONFLICT ☐
8. CONTROL THE MEETING ☐
9. DEVELOP ACTION PLANS/ITEMS AND MAKE
   ASSIGNMENTS ☐
10. END MEETING ON TIME ☐

FOLLOW-UP ON THE MEETING

Figure 7.2

satisfactory answer, don't hold the meeting. If a meeting does not have a clear purpose or objective(s), it usually lacks direction and a lot of time is wasted. Examples of meeting objectives are:

- To identify ways of increasing productivity.
- To discuss and identify solutions to a specific problem.
- To decide on how the new training programme will be implemented.
- To produce an action plan for the start-up of a new project.

Once you have established your objective you may find there is a better way of accomplishing it than through a meeting.

2. Identify the decisions/actions you want taken as a result of the meeting.
If you think about the meeting in advance and identify the decisions or actions you want taken, you are more likely to be successful in achieving them. Examples of decisions or actions you might want taken for the above objectives are:

- A list of actions for increasing productivity that you can present to your boss.
- A list of possible solutions to the problem with the recommended solution.
- An implementation plan for the new training programme.
- A completed action plan including the assignment of responsibilities for the new project.

3. Develop the agenda.
Many of the factors that make meetings ineffective can be traced to poor preparation. The key to meeting preparation is an agenda. The reasons why an agenda is so important are given in Figure 7.3.

When you develop the agenda you need to do the following.

- Focus on the purposes or objective(s) of the meeting, then identify the main topics for discussion. These should be geared to the achievement of the meeting purpose or objective(s).

AGENDA – PURPOSES

- Forces the meeting leader to prepare
- Encourages participants to prepare
- Provides structure for meetings – less chance of digressions and timewasting
- Ensures that all business is covered
- Improves management of time in meeting
- Puts the focus on meeting productivity

Figure 7.3

- Decide who are the most appropriate people to report on specific topics.

- Consider the objectives and topics of the meeting and invite the smallest number of appropriate people. Attendance at meetings too easily becomes customary, yet the usefulness of meetings tends to be in inverse proportion to the attendance and large meetings are less effective in thinking and decision-making than small team meetings. They are also much more expensive. It seems obvious that a meeting which involves 20 people is twice as expensive as one that involves 10 but that simple arithmetic is often ignored and people have to sit in meetings where much of the discussion is of no interest or use to them. Those people for whom the meeting would be a waste of time are better employed, and often would be happier, getting on with their jobs.

- Decide how long the meeting will take. To do this, estimate the length of time needed for each topic. Allow for an adequate discussion of topics and of Any Other Business at the end of the meeting.

- Choose the date and the start and finish times for the meeting. As well as looking at your own calendar, keep the needs of participants in mind and check for their availability at that time.

MEETING AGENDA

Name of department/unit:_____

Meeting called by:_____

Date:_____

Start/end times:_____

Place:_____

Meeting members:_____

_____

Preparation: _____

_____

_____

AGENDA ITEMS	PERSON(S) REPORTING	APPROX. TIMES
1.		
2.		
3.		
4.		
5.		
6.		
7.		
8.		
9.		
10.		

Individual action items: _____

_____

_____

_____

_____

Figure 7.4

● Book the meeting room for that date and time and arrange for any equipment or refreshments.

A sample agenda form that you might use for your meetings is shown in Figure 7.4

4. Send participants copies of the agenda.
Inform all the meeting participants by distributing an itemized agenda so that the topics to be discussed are clear and everyone can prepare. When everyone needs to prepare or bring along something, you can indicate this under 'preparation' on the meeting agenda. Circulate the agenda in advance and check with staff members who are reporting on specific topics to clarify their roles.

5. Prepare for your own topics and responsibilities.
Prepare your statement of the meeting's purpose or objective(s) and any other opening remarks. Then prepare for the topics you will introduce or report on. Consider the decisions and actions you want taken and how you might accomplish them.

6. Check any visual aids you plan to use.
Problems with visual aids and equipment can ruin any meeting or presentation. Overhead transparencies get mixed up, slides are upside down, the VCR and the monitor prove incompatible. If you are going to use visual aids in the meeting or make a presentation, REHEARSE. Check your equipment is working and the room set-up is adequate. (For suggestions on the preparation of visual aids see Appendix: How to Develop and Use Training or Presentation Aids.

Ten commandments for managing meetings

1. Start the meeting on time
The biggest complaint that people have about meetings is that they begin late. Be there 10 minutes before the beginning of the meeting to do any last-minute checks, chat with participants and break the ice. You might allow a few minutes leeway but start

close to the announced time so that you don't punish the people who arrived on time or encourage people to come late. Most members of a meeting keep their eyes on the leader, especially at the beginning. As you make your opening remarks, be aware of your posture (erect, positive, dominant) and of your facial expressions (lively, interested, encouraging). Your body language will often impress more than what you say.

2. State your meeting objective(s) clearly.
Give the reasons for the meeting, then briefly review the agenda and any 'ground rules' for the meeting, eg, no smoking.

3. Keep records of the meeting.
Assign someone to keep 'the minutes' so that you can focus on managing the meeting. Ideas, problems, solutions, actions to be taken, can be recorded on a flipchart. When someone is taking 'the minutes' on the flipchart this provides a focus for discussion and points can be clarified as they arise. Everyone can see what's been decided, the potential solutions and the actions that should be taken.

4. Ensure adequate discussion of the topics.
An atmosphere of free exchange can only be created when participants see that you really want their opinions and ideas. You can encourage participation through the skilful use of questions and invite reluctant or silent participants to join in.

● Use 'open-ended questions' and a questioning tone to show you really want to know what people think, will listen to their ideas, and are open to change. For example:

'What do you think are some possible solutions to this situation?'

● Ask 'overhead questions' to the group as a whole, especially when you want to start a discussion or check that everyone's had their 'say'. For example:

'Before we move on, are there any other comments or thoughts on this point?'

Avoid asking overhead questions when time is short and you want to limit general discussion.

• Ask 'direct questions' to selected individuals to invite them into the discussion and 'close down' participants who may be dominating the discussion or repeating the same points. For example:

'Keith, how do you think this might affect your operation?'

Direct questions are best used when participants are comfortable and engaged in the discussion. They can seem threatening at the beginning of a meeting.

5. *Push the meeting along towards decisions and actions.*
Follow the agenda and keep the meeting focused on each topic in turn. When 'hidden agendas' and personal issues surface, bring the discussion back to the agenda topic. Move from discussing ideas towards discussion of how things can be done. A statement like 'That's an interesting idea, but how would you do it?', encourages the group to consider actions and the implementation of ideas.

6. *Manage the use of time.*
Avoid spending time on trivial items at the expense of the important ones. If you indicate times for each item on the agenda, this will help. Especially in budget discussions avoid Parkinson's Law of Triviality which states:

The time spent on any item of the agenda will be in inverse proportion to the sum involved. C. N. Parkinson, *Parkinson's Law.*

Parkinson's Law of Triviality of course applies to other matters as well as money. You may, however, want people to argue about the trivial items and ignore the big issues – Machiavellian meeting strategy is not discussed in this chapter!

7. *Manage conflict.*

Meeting leaders often see conflict as a danger to themselves and to the success of their meeting. In order to make good decisions though, you need a healthy confict of ideas. If everyone agrees, then proposals which should be criticized or at least examined more carefully are not. Great blunders have been made because people in meetings were afraid to be 'too critical' or to ask what they felt was an 'obvious' or 'stupid' question.

Personal conflicts that surface during a meeting can be very destructive. Often they arise through differences in participants' background, knowledge and experience. These differences can, however, be a source of strength if you handle them in a positive way. After all, the team leader's job is to blend the different knowledge, experience and ideas of team members.

If conflict does arise, don't take sides. Look for compromises and find, and build on, areas for agreement. You might say: 'Could you each take a few minutes to explain your thoughts on the subject. Then we'll compare your views. Would anyone like to start off the discussion?' Occasionally you may find that opponents have been saying the same thing differently and are actually in agreement.

If a conflict continues, suggest that those with conflicting views have a separate meeting later to discuss the situation.

8. *Control the meeting.*

In order to resolve the conflicting demands of full and free discussion and the achievement of decisions and actions, you must be seen to be firmly and positively in charge without being bullying. In particular, make sure there is only one meeting going on – discourage any side discussions and off-topic discussions during the meeting.

You should also be alert for signs that indicate something needs improving. 'Read' the meeting members – their facial expressions and body language, the tone of their comments, the general atmosphere of the meeting. When there is too little interaction and people seem bored, generate discussion. When there is too much interaction and some people seem confused, keep things focused and summarize progress.

9. Develop action plans/items and make assignments.
Following the discussion of each topic on the agenda, clarify any action(s) that need to be taken, people's responsibilities and their assignments. Make sure these are recorded.

10. End the meeting on time.
The second biggest complaint people have about meetings is that they don't finish on time. At the end restate the purpose or objective(s) of the meeting, summarize what has been accomplished and review any action agreed upon. If a flipchart was used to record the minutes, you or the person who took the minutes can use the flipchart to review.

At some meetings you may be the leader responsible for preparing and conducting the meeting. At other times – when you attend meetings with your boss or other managers – you are a meeting participant. This chapter has focused on leader skills but meeting effectiveness depends also upon the preparation and techniques used by meeting participants. Ten Commandments For Meeting Participants are given in Figure 7.5.

TEN COMMANDMENTS FOR MEETING PARTICIPANTS

1. Prepare for the meeting
2. Be on time.
3. Listen and contribute to discussions
4. Present your arguments clearly and concisely
5. Be open-minded and receptive to others' contributions
6. Stay on the agenda and on the subject
7. Avoid getting involved in side conversations
8. Ask questions to clarify points and ensure that everyone understands
9. Take well-organized notes on your Action Items
10. Take action or follow-up on your Action Items

Figure 7.5

Follow-up on the meeting

● Ensure that 'the minutes' or some other record of the meeting are distributed. This responsibility may be delegated to the person who acted as recorder.

● Complete your own action items.

● Evaluate your own effectiveness and the effectiveness of the meeting. Look at the Guidelines for Effective Meetings Checklist and ask yourself: 'What things went well, and why?', 'Where did I have problems, and why?', 'What can I do differently next time?'

● Follow-up and check that staff have completed their action items.

Common situations

Situation: One of your people wants to argue with you and is beginning to disrupt the meeting.
Response: Refer to the agenda and the need to move ahead. Say you will discuss the issue in private afterwards. Then use questions to involve other participants and listen to their views.

Situation: One of your people tends to dominate the meetings.
Response: Ask for other people's contributions and, if necessary, use direct questions to draw them out. Avoid eye contact with the 'dominator' because when you catch a person's eye, it gives him or her permission to intervene.

Situation: One person starts a side conversation with neighbours.
Response: This is more likely to occur in large meetings. A talkative person may want to speak when the group is listening to someone else, or a more cautious person may want to try out an idea before presenting it to the whole group. Side conversations are inevitable in meetings and are usually brief. They become a problem if prolonged. One technique you can use is to invite the person to share with everyone what is being said.

Another way to handle this situation is simply to be quiet and look at the person. Generally this will stop the side conversation.

Situation: A controversial or touchy subject arises which only senior management can deal with.
Response: Do not promise to get the 'right' action from management, but only to report the views and suggestions given at the meeting.

Action items

Prepare for your next meeting using the Effective Meeting Guidelines (Figure 7.2) and the Agenda form (Figure 7.4).

CHAPTER 8

How to Delegate Work and Responsibilities

> 'Tom appeared on the side-walk with a bucket of whitewash and a longhandled brush. He surveyed the fence, and the gladness went out of his nature, and a deep melancholy settled down upon his spirit. Thirty yards of broad fence nine feet high! . . . At this dark and hopeless moment an inspiration burst upon him. Nothing less than a great, magnificent inspiration'. Mark Twain, *The Adventures of Tom Sawyer*.

Tom's magnificent inspiration is to persuade the other boys to whitewash the fence. He gets them to do his job by convincing them that whitewashing is enjoyable, can only be done by skilled people and requires a high standard of performance. Tom therefore gets the fence whitewashed by using some classic delegation techniques.

Delegation, however, is not just a matter of getting rid of the jobs you don't want to do yourself. Delegation should be done for more positive reasons and for developing others.

Delegation is also not assigning work to people that they should already be doing. When you delegate you give people responsibilities or tasks which are new to them. This chapter focuses on the benefits of delegation and how you can make maximum use of your people's knowledge, skills, experience and interests. The objective of this chapter is to help you delegate appropriate tasks and projects to your staff.

Your current situation

Take a few minutes to consider how you are delegating to the people who report to you. First list the people who report to you. Then indicate the tasks or projects you have delegated to them most recently. You could use a form like the one shown in Figure 8.1.

DELEGATION RECORD	
Staff Members	Delegated Tasks/Projects

Figure 8.1

Who has not been delegated to?

Why?

Why delegation is important

The assignment of work to others is essential in every organization and delegation is a fundamental aspect of every manager's and supervisor's job. If you fail to delegate effectively, you have to work harder and may often feel self-righteous about having to 'do everything'. You may well make more mistakes and accomplish less than managers who delegate and use the skills and experience of their people. The lack of meaningful delegation may also lead to your people losing interest in the job and not accomplishing very much.

Managers give many reasons for not delegating. Here's a list of the most common, some of which you may recognize. Below each reason is a response.

● *'I'm so busy I don't have enough time to delegate'.*
Response: If you don't have enough time, this means you should be delegating more.

● *'I usually do that job myself'.*
Response: Many new managers are afraid of losing a familiar part of the job – often something they did before they were promoted and which they were praised for. Now though, as a manager, you need to look at the jobs you 'usually' do, and see if someone else can benefit from learning how to do them.

● *'I like doing that job myself'.*
Response: Obviously you need to enjoy some of the jobs you do – you've got your own motivation to think about. But don't keep all the interesting or stimulating jobs for yourself – your people would probably appreciate a change from *their* routine.

● *'I don't have enough people'.*
Response: Look at your own and your staff workloads. What are the unnecessary or low-priority jobs you can dispense with? If you really don't have enough people, put together a justification for more staff.

● *'My people aren't skilled enough'.*
Response: You need to develop your people's skills systematically through training and appropriate work assignments. Use delegation as one means of developing their skills and building up their experience. Make sure though that assignments are within your

people's capabilities and that you are providing enough support, either yourself or from other people, to make them successful.

- *'If I delegate, they'll make mistakes'.*
Response: Your people may make some mistakes but mistakes are a necessary part of learning and often a stimulus to improvement. The mistakes should not be serious if you have delegated properly and monitored their progress with the assignment. More mistakes are likely to be made if you don't delegate. And you're the one who is likely to be making them because you're spreading your effort too thinly.

- *'If I delegate, they'll make the decisions'.*
Response: Many managers fear a loss of authority, especially if that authority was hard-gained. When you delegate a job to someone, you should allow him or her to make the routine operational decisions and then discuss the more critical policy-related decisions together. Your boss will probably hold you accountable for the task or project so the responsibility for final decision-making still lies with you. In order to safeguard your interests and to provide guidance you need to monitor the person's progress with the assignment. The amount of monitoring will of course depend upon the experience and trustworthiness of the person you have delegated to.

- *'I don't know how to delegate'.*
Response: Read on. Don't expect all the answers, though. Delegation, like any other management or supervisory responsibility, is not an easy process. You need to tailor the Delegation Guidelines (Figure 8.2) to the staff member and the situation.

Benefits of effective delegation

What's in it for you
Effective delegation will achieve the following.

- Give you the time you need to think and to do your own job as a manager better. In particular, delegation increases your time for important managerial functions like planning, organizing and developing your people.

● Give you time to concentrate on the tasks that your own boss delegates to you – those important tasks and projects that require your special knowledge and expertise.

● Improve the quality of your decision-making because staff may have better information than you on specific aspects of a task or project.

● Increase staff productivity. A delegated task provides your staff member with a Priority A so that he or she is not preoccupied with Priority Cs, trivial tasks that occupy time but don't contribute significantly to the success of the operation.

● Help you to assess individual staff performance when the time comes for performance review. You and the staff member can discuss performance on the tasks or projects that have been delegated during the assessment period.

● Enable you to assess the potential that someone has for a job other than the one they are doing at present. You can assess their competence and promotability – how well the staff member writes letters, conducts meetings, works with other staff and clients.

Delegation allows you to make maximum use of the staff available to you. Unlike machinery, people become more valuable the more they are used. If you are developing your staff, they should become more valuable as time goes on – worth more this year than they were last year. Delegation therefore gives you an opportunity to expand your people's capabilities and use them to better effect.

What's in it for your staff
Effective delegation will achieve the following.

● Demonstrate your trust and confidence in your staff's abilities. Responsibility tends to motivate people and increase job satisfaction and effectiveness.

● Improve staff morale because it shows that you aren't keeping all the interesting or important jobs for yourself.

● Give staff a chance to use their initiative and learn through their involvement in some decision-making and problem-solving.

● Develop people for larger or different jobs from the ones they are doing now. Delegation should stretch (but not break) the abilities of your staff and give them space to grow.

Delegation guidelines

The basic steps in delegating a task or project are shown in Figure 8.2. These steps are shown in the form of a checklist to make them easy to use. The notes below are intended to give further information and suggestions on how to follow these guidelines.

Preparation

1. Identify the assignment to delegate.
You need to identify a task or project which someone can work on after adequate briefing but with the minimum of supervision and monitoring. Think through all aspects of the assignment to make it as meaningful and challenging as possible. Think of delegating the following.

- The job *you* used to do before you were promoted. Make sure that you aren't trying to do your new job and your old job, which you may have enjoyed, as well.
- Routine operational tasks that you do because you've always done them.
- Special projects that require more time and concentrated effort than you can devote to them.
- A part of your work or part of a job that you want the person to work on, learn about or get some experience in.

DELEGATION GUIDELINES

PREPARATION
1. IDENTIFY ASSIGNMENT ☐

2. SURVEY STAFF WORKLOADS ☐

3. SELECT APPROPRIATE PERSON ☐

4. SCHEDULE MEETING ☐

MEETING
1. ESTABLISH CLIMATE FOR TWO WAY
   COMMUNICATION ☐

2. OUTLINE ASSIGNMENT,
   RESPONSIBILITIES, AND AUTHORITY ☐

3. DISCUSS ASSIGNMENT AND AGREE
   COMPLETION DATES ☐

FOLLOW-UP
1. MONITOR AND REINFORCE
   PERFORMANCE ☐

2. PROVIDE ADDITIONAL INFORMATION
   OR SUPPORT ☐

3. EVALUATE RESULTS AND GIVE
   FEEDBACK ☐

Figure 8.2

There are however some assignments that you should not delegate. Avoid delegating the following.

- Jobs that have been specifically given to you by your manager. You may, however, delegate parts of the task, eg, collecting information or preparing material for a report.
- Work which involves major policy recommendations, changes in overall strategy or in the direction of the organization.
- Jobs that require the use of your authority or job level, eg, approval of expenditure, your presence at a meeting, dealing with someone at your own level or above or matters that require your signature.
- Personnel decisions like recruitment and confidential matters like staff appraisal or discipline.
- The handling of crisis situations. Your people should be able to handle certain aspects of the crisis (decide which) but you need to retain overall control and responsibility.

2. Survey staff workloads.
Have some of your people got too much to do and others too little? Are some of them doing only routine tasks, while others do all the new work? Try to ensure that each person has a balanced workload. A mix of routine tasks together with a special project provides a blend of the familiar and something new and challenging.

3. Select the appropriate person for the assignment.
Look for the qualified or potentially qualified person who needs to learn a new task. Analyse that person's workload to ensure that he or she has enough time to do the new task and if not, consider some reassignment of tasks/projects.

4. Schedule a meeting with the person to discuss the assignment.

Meeting

1. Establish a climate for two way communication.
Discuss with your staff member his or her current workload.

Changes in workload may involve a certain amount of negotiation and give and take on both sides is necessary.

2. Outline the assignment, responsibilities, and authority.

Explain the task or project you are delegating and make the specific goals very clear. Describe what's happening at the moment on this task/project or why this new job needs to be done. Explain what benefits there will be and why this person's personal qualifications, skills and experience will be useful. Highlight the challenging aspects of the task. At this stage you should also define any specific limitations of time, money and resources.

Delegating, however, is more than giving instructions. Effective delegation requires that you give the staff member the necessary information and authority to do the job. Let the person know that he or she has the power to act and exercise initiative on routine operational matters. Tell the person that you will also let everyone concerned know about the authority and responsibilities you have given so that confusion is minimized.

3. Discuss the assignment and agree completion dates.

Through discussion you show respect for and tap into your staff member's reservoir of knowledge and experience. Use questions like:

'Well I've done most of the talking so far. What are your views?'

'Do you see any problems with this?'

'Are there any other things we could try?'

Your questioning should encourage the person to think about the assignment and let him or her know that they will be making some choices. In this way you can increase their involvement and commitment to the assignment.

You may also need to negotiate with your staff member at this point and discuss the new assignment in terms of his or her current workload. Try to avoid using your 'position power' to squeeze unreasonable objectives and deadlines out of the person

– if he or she fails because of unrealistic expectations, you will be responsible. Differences in style may also create problems . If you're a 'go for it' boss and are delegating to a person with a more 'considered' approach, you may lose patience with what you regard as procrastination. Similarly a 'go for it' staff member may think your considered approach too tentative and want more 'direction'.

At the end of the discussion you might ask the person to restate the assignment so as to ensure that everything is clear and to encourage commitment. Make sure also that the staff member has the information and resources necessary to do the job, or knows where to get them. The required results of this assignment, the deadlines and the staff member's accountability also need to be clear or there may well be difficulties in future.

Follow-Up

1. Monitor and reinforce performance.
Don't supervise too closely but do establish reporting procedures and times. It's necessary to have adequate control, but staff are better developed and motivated when controls are exercised through objective-setting, establishing measurable standards and being delegated the authority to work within this framework.

2. Provide additional information or support as needed.
Use coaching techniques (see Chapter 9, How to Coach your People) and encourage two-way communication on the progress of the assignment.

3. Evaluate results and give feedback.
Delegation is intended to develop people as well as get the job done. Make sure you give feedback and provide some recognition for success.

Delegation form

The delegation form, Figure 8.3, can be used to help you organize your delegation of tasks and projects. First, complete the form in draft in preparation for the delegation meeting. Then, using the information given by the staff member, add notes to the form during the meeting, eg, additional action items, completion dates agreed on, names of people who might assist, any training required.

Here are suggestions on how you might complete the different sections and use this form.

Current workload.
The jobs which the person is already doing. Based on information from the staff member you may need to add to this. Ensure that the person doesn't already have more work than he or she can handle.

Delegated task/project.
The name of the task/project or a brief description of it.

Task/project completion date.
When does this task/project need to be completed? If there's no absolute deadline, then put a provisional one which can be discussed at the meeting.

Background/current status of task/project.
What has been happening with this task/project? Is it new, or has someone already been working on it? What was the last thing that happened related to this task/project?

Early action items.
What needs to be done *soon* by you and the staff member to move on with this task/project? Who needs to be contacted, what plans need to be made, what action needs to be taken? Any training that is needed should be identified and built into the plan, eg, attendance at a project management course, computer training, etc. Completion dates need to be given for each action item so that the task/project can move ahead systematically and both you and the staff member know what will be done and when.

DELEGATION FORM

Staff Member:_____

Current workload.*Add to this based on information from the staff member:*_____

_____

_____

_____

_____

Name or brief description of delegated task/project:

_____

_____

_____

_____

_____

Task/project completion date:_____

Background/current status of task/project:_____

_____

_____

_____

_____

Early Action items with completion dates. *What needs to be done soon?*

1._____

_____

_____

2._____

_____

_____

3._____

_____

4._____

Figure 8.3

DELEGATION FORM

Task/project milestones - major stages in this project with completion dates:

1._____

2._____

3._____

4._____

Other staff involved and their responsibilities.
Who else is involved or needs to be involved? What might they be able to do to help?

1._____

2._____

3._____

Additional notes. *Anything else that arises from the discussion or needs to be remembered:*

_____
_____
_____
_____
_____
_____

Date task/project delegated:_____

Date of task/project review meeting: _____

Figure 8.3 *(cont)*

Task/project milestones.
What are the major stages in this project and when should each stage be completed? This is the long-term planning aspect of delegation.

Other staff involved and their responsibilities.
Who else is involved or needs to be involved? What might these people be able to do? Based upon your discussion with the staff member, especially discussion of the current workload, you might assign additional help. The staff member might also know of someone who has particular expertise or interest in this assignment. You might also see involvement as a developmental activity for another member of staff. If other people are going to be involved, make sure you inform them and that individual responsibilities are clearly defined.

Additional notes.
Include anything else that arises from the discussion or needs to be remembered. Make sure you discuss the person's ideas for completing the assignment. Any problems that arise should be noted here.

Date task/project delegated.
The date of your meeting.

Date of task/project review meeting.
Arrange for another formal meeting, perhaps for a date after the early action items have been completed.

Complete the form with the additional information as a record of the meeting and the task/project status. You can then give a copy of the final form to the staff member for his or her future reference.

Common situations

Situation: Your staff member faces some difficulties and tries to delegate the assignment back to you or other members of staff.
Response: Diplomatically say 'No'. Tell the person that the assignment is his or hers to handle. Ask the staff member to think about the difficulties and tell you how they should be handled. What are the alternatives? Determine together what the next move will be and who will make it. Make sure that you don't commit yourself to making moves that your staff member could make.

When further support is needed, arrange to meet with the staff member at appointed times to discuss the next action. Increasing the level of supervision, however, is not a good solution to delegation problems and you should avoid supervising too closely.

Situation: You find yourself always delegating to the same person because he or she seems to have the most skills and be most dependable.
Response: There's a tendency for managers to always delegate to the person with most skills or the person they *trust*. The better people are therefore 'rewarded' with more work and the weaker people with less. You need to spread delegation around to different people in order to get a greater number of staff trained and gain a better assessment of their capabilities. The person with most skills and experience could be used as a team leader or asked to work on a task or project with one of your new or weaker members of staff.

Situation: You have delegated a specific project but are not happy about progress. You don't know whether to step in and correct the situation yourself.
Response: Meet with the person and discuss progress on the project. Work together to identify the problems and how they might be rectified. Identify specifically what needs to be done and when. If necessary you might ask the person to put together an action plan based on your discussion. Make sure that you don't take on responsibility for tasks which the person you have delegated to could perform.

Situation: The assignment is not completed on time and a lot of additional work needs to be done to bring it up to standard.

Response: Prepare for a coaching session with your staff member. As part of the preparation, ask yourself some questions. Did I assume too much of this person? Did he or she have enough knowledge, skills, experience to handle the assignment? Did he or she need more support and follow-up? Look at what's been done on the assignment so far and list the things that still need to be done. These should be the focus of your coaching session (see Chapter 9 on How to Coach your People).

Action items

Ensure that appropriate projects and tasks are delegated to your staff by answering the following questions.

1. What task or project are you presently doing that could be delegated?

2. Who could this task or project be delegated to?

3. What difficulties do you foresee in delegating this task or project?

4. How might these difficulties be overcome?

CHAPTER 9
How to Coach Your People

'Coaching is face-to-face leadership that pulls together people with diverse backgrounds, talents, experiences and interests, encourages them to step up to responsibility and continued achievement, and treats them as full-scale partners and contributors'. Tom Peters and Nancy Austin, *A Passion For Excellence*.

Coaching is the everyday process of working with employees and helping them to improve their skills and performance. Sometimes your coaching might involve training and showing someone how to perform a new task. At other times it might be developmental and concerned with helping a person develop their skills in working on a task or project. Coaching, however, is most difficult when it involves correction – when you are dealing with mistakes or problems and helping an employee to improve their performance.

You probably already coach extensively. You use your own personal experience, knowledge and understanding to help your staff work on projects, reach decisions, learn how to cope with new situations and handle problems and mistakes.

The purpose of this chapter is to strengthen the good things that you are already doing and to outline a systematic approach to coaching sessions.

Your current situation

Communication is one of the most important aspects of your job. Coaching in particular is a test of your knowledge about communication and your communication skills. The question-

COMMUNICATION QUESTIONNAIRE			
Number	Statement	True	False
1.	Communication is a fairly simple process		
2.	If an instruction is clearly understood, it will nearly always be carried out		
3.	People often communicate without realizing it		
4.	Listening well comes naturally to most people		
5.	Just listening to problems does little good unless you can offer the person some good advice		
6.	Intelligent people should understand a message the first time		
7.	A person who asks a lot of questions does not understand as clearly as a person who asks only a few questions		
8.	When people do not understand a message, they nearly always tell you so.		
9.	Repeating what a person has said is a good check to see if you understood the message properly		
10.	The way a person stands or sits is an important form of communication		
11.	A person's facial expression can change the meaning of the words spoken		
12.	Nodding your head up and down while listening usually indicates interest		
13.	Stating a point loudly and frequently is often the most effective way to make it understood		
14.	A person who really disagrees may say he or she agrees only to avoid further argument		
15.	Effective communication seldom takes place between people who are angry		

Figure 9.1

naire in Figure 9.1 checks your general knowledge of communication and is intended to make you think about your coaching skills. Indicate whether you think the following statements are true or false.

Your responses

1. *False.* Large amounts of time and money are wasted because of the confusion and misunderstandings that arise due to faulty communication.

2. *True.* Instructions are often not clearly understood.

3. *True.* Our body language, particularly facial expression and tone of voice, often communicates more than our words.

4. *False.* Rather than listening to others we often focus our attention on what *we* are saying or about to say. Sometimes we prefer to interrupt rather than listen. We can improve the effectiveness of our coaching skills significantly by practising listening.

5. *False.* Your listening to people's problems can help them release pent-up frustrations and anxieties. The discussion can also help them to sort out or come to terms with their problems.

6. *False.* Intelligent people will often ask for more details or ask questions to clarify the message.

7. *False.* Questioning often indicates that the questioner needs more details or is particularly interested in the topic.

8. *False.* When people do not understand your message, they may feel too embarrassed or afraid to tell you.

9. *True.* Repeating or summarizing key points or feelings is a useful technique in coaching. It shows that you understand what the person is saying.

Statements 10–13 are all *true* and emphasize the importance of a person's body language in coaching sessions.

14. *True*. Good coaching involves the person being coached and tries to obtain his or her 'real' agreement to solutions or actions.

15. *True*. Effective communication depends on people listening to each other. Angry people often don't listen.

Why coaching is important

Coaching is important because if it's used effectively it leads to increased use of people's skills and improvements in individual job performance. Perhaps most important of all from the organizational point of view, effective coaching can prevent 'small problems' from developing into big ones. Your coaching can prevent minor work infractions or disagreements from leading to serious disciplinary actions and causes for resignation or dismissal. Such disciplinary actions and the loss of experienced people can waste a lot of time and money and be very expensive for the organization.

Coaching is often confused with counselling. Counselling is concerned with helping people to resolve personal problems, whereas coaching focuses on improving people's work performance. Coaching is therefore a management responsibility. If you find out that a personal problem is affecting someone's job performance, coaching may involve some counselling (depending upon your relationship with the person) but serious counselling should be dealt with by those with qualifications and experience in this area.

There are three types of coaching:

- *Instructional coaching* which relates to one-to-one training and is described in Chapter 3, Mentoring and On-the-job Training.
- *Developmental coaching* which involves your working with a person and giving him or her the benefit of your knowledge and experience. This is probably the most common coaching activity and often involves delegation. Chapter 8, How to

Delegate Work and Responsibilities, describes this form of coaching.

● *Corrective coaching* which focuses on helping people improve their work performance and handle problems or mistakes. This form of coaching is the main focus of this chapter.

Benefits of coaching

What's in it for you?

Coaching sessions can help you by providing the following.

● A tool for monitoring your operation and your people. Through coaching you can keep people 'on track' with their regular assignments and the special tasks or projects you have delegated to them.

● New sources of information and skills. You can learn from your people because good coaching involves two-way communication.

● Opportunities to develop and practise your own interpersonal and management skills

What's in it for the employee

Coaching benefits your people by providing the following.

● Regular help so that they can resolve work problems. Research has shown that employees are more than twice as willing to engage in coaching sessions as their coaches! If you coach constructively you can turn a mistake or work problem into a learning situation.

● Stimulus to someone who may just be cruising along. Coaching shows your interest in what the person is doing and your attention can improve their performance.

● Opportunities for people to develop their own problem-solving skills. A good coach doesn't impose solutions but through discussion helps people to sort out their own problems and make better decisions.

Coaching techniques

There is a wide range of coaching situations and you need to adjust your coaching style according to the situation and the experience of an employee in performing a particular job.

A *directive coaching style* tends to be most appropriate for new members of staff or those who are unfamiliar with a task or project. You may need to give specific instructions about what to do and monitor the person closely to provide support. A more directive style is also appropriate at those points in a coaching session where the person needs you to make decisions and give instructions.

A *participatory coaching style* is more appropriate when you are coaching experienced people who have done the particular type of task before and may require only general guidance and monitoring. Your coaching style here should focus more on joint problem-solving and providing general guidance rather than giving instructions. A participatory style is also more appropriate for the discussion and problem-solving parts of a coaching session.

As a participatory style involves more questioning and discussion, it obviously takes more time. The greater involvement of the staff member, however, leads to your making more informed decisions and to the person being more committed to change.

As mentioned above, the most difficult type of coaching is *corrective coaching* where you are trying to correct a problem or situation, or preventing a larger problem from arising. The rest of this chapter will focus on this.

Corrective coaching techniques

There are three key techniques that you can use to make your corrective coaching effective:

1. Descriptive statements

2. Questioning techniques
3. Body language.

1. Descriptive statements
What's the difference between these two statements?

1. Frank, you're always late for work . Can't you get up in the morning?
2. Frank, you've been late for work three times this week. You were 10 minutes late on Monday and 15 minutes late on Wednesday. This morning you were half an hour late. What's the matter?

The first statement is an evaluative statement. It focuses on Frank's character, judges him as lazy and would be experienced as a personal attack. The statement is also general with its use of 'always late' and Frank might easily be able to deny it: 'I'm not always late. I'm usually on time. You don't notice when I'm on time, or even when I stay late to finish work'. An argument would probably follow with Frank and his supervisor becoming more emotional.

The second statement is a descriptive statement. It describes Frank's behaviour and is factual and specific, referring to particular occurrences. Frank cannot easily deny the truth of the second statement and by focusing on behaviour, the statement is not a personal attack. A reasonable discussion of the problem would probably follow.

The key point here is that:

People can't change their personalities but they can change their behaviour.

Figure 9.2 compares evaluative and descriptive statements.

2. Questioning techniques
Good coaching helps people to learn and through your questioning you can show people how to ask questions of themselves. This makes them think more deeply about what they are doing

EVALUATIVE AND DESCRIPTIVE STATEMENTS COMPARED	
EVALUATIVE STATEMENTS	DESCRIPTIVE STATEMENTS
Focus on the person, express judgements and are often experienced as a personal attack.	Focus on the person's actions and behaviour. They do not attack him or her personally.
Are easy to use because they are based on general impressions.	Require some investment of time and effort to gather the facts.
Are general and vague. They may involve exaggeration and use absolutes such as 'all', 'none', 'always', 'never'. A person can often easily refute these general statements.	Are factual and specific. They refer to particular instances or occurrences with dates. A person cannot easily refute these statements.
Do not improve performance because no specific directions are given.	Improve performance because specific directions are given.
Damage the relationship between you and the person.	Can strengthen the relationship between you and the person because he or she receives feedback that helps him or her solve problems.

Figure 9.2

EVALUATIVE AND DESCRIPTIVE STATEMENTS

Convert the following evaluative statements into descriptive statements.

1. This work is sloppy. Why did you make so many mistakes?

   _____

2. You don't take enough responsibility or show enough initiative.

   _____

3. You are always having arguments with other members of staff. You should learn to get along with the other people.

   _____

4. You seem to be spending a lot of time away from the job.

   _____

Figure 9.3

and why, and about alternative courses of action and their implications.

Just as you should avoid evaluative statements, avoid critical or personal questions. Use open-ended questions – questions that begin with what, when, where, how and who and can't be answered by simple statements or yes/no answers. Open-ended questions are good for drawing out feelings and attitudes, encouraging people to expand on points and for provoking thought. Open-ended questions are especially useful in getting people who are silent or upset to open up. They also ensure you find out as much as possible and don't do most of the talking.

Two types of open question you can use in coaching sessions are:

- Information questions
- Thought–provoking questions

Information questions are used to ask for additional information and are particularly useful in the early coaching steps when you are trying to assess the situation. Some examples are: 'What happened . . .?', 'What time . . .?', 'Why did you . . ?'

Thought-provoking questions are used to encourage the person to think through the problem and to explore alternative solutions and actions. These questions are used particularly in the later coaching steps. Examples of thought-provoking questions are: 'What do you think we can do about this problem?', 'What do you think is better?', 'What do you think are the options?', 'What is the best choice?'

When you have asked a question, wait for the person to respond. Avoid answering your own questions.

3. Body language
Various researchers over the years have established the impact of body language as being between 60 and 80 per cent of any communication. Several statements in the questionnaire in Figure 9.1 referred to the importance of body language in communication and coaching. Figure 9.4 gives some suggestions on how to physically communicate in coaching sessions so that your body language reinforces what you say.

Coaching guidelines

The basic steps in conducting a coaching session are shown in Figure 9.5. These Coaching Guidelines are given in a checklist form to make them easy to use. The notes below give further information on each of the steps and provide suggestions on how to conduct the session.

BODY LANGUAGE IN COACHING

Posture

Sit facing the person and leaning forward a little to listen. Stay relatively relaxed and avoid fidgeting.

Gestures

Nod your head occasionally to encourage contributions, show interest and understanding.
Use your hands for emphasis especially when describing steps or actions that might be taken.
Avoid outward signs of boredom like yawning or watching the clock.

Facial expressions

Maintain reasonable eye contact. Looking away or down at the desk communicates anxiety.
Show understanding with an attentive expression and a genuine smile.

Voice

Keep your voice even when making descriptive statements. Try to maintain a relaxed and varied tone during the discussion.
Use a questioning tone when discussing possible solutions. Make your voice stronger and more emphatic when you agree upon future action.

Figure 9.4

1. *Based on the facts of the situation, state the problem exactly and clearly.*
Welcome the person at the beginning of the session. Then describe the problem which has led to this coaching session. Particularly at the beginning of the session, it's important to be objective and factual and to use descriptive rather than evaluative

---

COACHING GUIDELINES

1. STATE THE PROBLEM EXACTLY AND CLEARLY. ☐

2. REACH AGREEMENT THAT PROBLEM EXISTS. ☐

3. DISCUSS CAUSES OF PROBLEM. ☐

4. DISCUSS POSSIBLE SOLUTIONS AND
   AGREE ACTIONS ☐

5. DOCUMENT THE COACHING SESSION. ☐

6. FOLLOW-UP ON COACHING SESSION. ☐

Figure 9.5

statements. Don't jump to conclusions, and right at the beginning you need to find out whether this problem may be the result of a misunderstanding or personal problems, maybe at home.

2. Reach agreement that a problem exists.
One way of gaining agreement is to point out the gap between the standard and the person's actions and behaviour. For example, 'It's a company rule that we're here at 8 o'clock', 'The Operating Plan was due by July 5', 'The standard is only 5 per cent

wastage'. Another way to gain agreement is to describe the consequences for the operation, for other people and for the person if this problem continues. Obtaining someone's agreement that a problem exists is the most important and often the most difficult step in the corrective coaching process. If you continue without gaining agreement, additional difficulties will arise and you may need to go back again to try to secure agreement. Once you have it, emphasize that agreement so that it's clear to the person and he or she can't go back on it later.

3. Discuss causes of the problem.
Determine the facts by asking information questions like 'What happened . . .', 'What time . . .', 'Why did you do that?' During this step, you should encourage the person to talk about the problem while you listen and try to see the situation from his or her point of view. Too much sympathy, however, may encourage the person to exaggerate difficulties and distort the account of their causes. Watch out also for any over-protective feelings or needs within yourself to be liked and appreciated. Recognize your own personal feelings as they relate to the issue and share those feelings with the other person.

In addition to your use of questions, you can provide structure for the coaching session by interrupting occasionally and using reflective statements like: 'So you think that . . .', 'Does this mean that . . .'. These statements reflect back to the person the picture he or she is presenting and check your understanding of what has been said. They can also stimulate the person to expand the point or help you to guide him or her to the next stage in the coaching session.

4. Discuss possible solutions and agree upon action(s).
You need to guide the discussion from describing or talking about the past to talking about the future: from talking about things that have gone wrong to how to prevent them from going wrong again. Use thought-provoking questions that direct the person towards the future like: 'What do you think you can do about this problem?', 'Have you considered . . . ?', 'What do you think would happen if . . .'.

You may need to narrow down the possible solutions or actions by discussing two or more options: 'What do you think would be better . . .?' The responsibility for a person changing his or her behaviour is not yours: it lies with the individual. This is why the person needs to be involved in making decisions and agreeing upon future action. In this way, he or she will also be more committed to these decisions or actions. On the basis that people generally respond well to personal information, you might tell the person something about how you see things and your own experience related to this problem. This demonstrates your own involvement as a person rather than someone judging from 'on high'.

If necessary, refer the person to other people who have special knowledge or indicate other sources of information. You might also consider the range of motivational options that you can use to bring about improved performance. Perhaps increased responsibility and recognition may have a role in stimulating improvement.

End the session on an encouraging note and agree on a target for future performance. You might arrange to discuss the issue again at a future date to provide support and monitor progress.

5. *Document the session.*
You need to document the session – perhaps write a brief memo for the employee's file. Then you will have a record to refer back to later, particularly if there are any further coaching sessions. Document the solutions or actions agreed upon and the follow-up date.

6. *Follow-up on the session.*
Consider how and when you might follow-up on the coaching session – tomorrow, next week, next month? How will you recognize achievement or change? What will you do if the problem continues?

Coaching preparation form

If you want your corrective coaching to be effective, you need to prepare. You need to mentally rehearse what will happen in the session and be ready for any problems which may arise. Serious corrective coaching shouldn't be done on an impulse and without preparation.

The Coaching Preparation Form, Figure 9.6, will help you plan and conduct coaching sessions. The notes below explain how you can use the form.

Person to be coached.
Identify the person to be coached. Always arrange to coach people individually even if more than one person is involved. Don't reprimand people in public.

Place.
Arrange the meeting for a place where there will be few interruptions or distractions.

Date/start and finish times.
Identify the date and the start and finish times for the coaching session. Make sure you allow yourself sufficient time especially when doing corrective coaching. Coaching sessions may require up to 45 minutes and should focus on only one or two issues.

Facts of the situation.
Use descriptive statements which describe the facts of the situation, project or problem. Try to be objective in recording what actually happened.

Your objectives for the session. What do you want to achieve?
Write down what you want the person to do as a result of the coaching session. During the meeting you should move from discussing the past to talking about the person's future performance. It's not enough to write 'improved performance' as an objective. You need to identify specific ways in which performance should improve, how the improvement will be shown and by when.

COACHING PREPARATION FORM

Person to be coached:_____

Place:_____

Date: _____

Start and finish times:_____

Facts of the situation. Use descriptive statements:

_____

_____

_____

_____

_____

Objectives for the session – what you want to achieve:

_____

_____

_____

_____

1. State the problem exactly and clearly. Use descriptive statements:

_____

_____

_____

_____

_____

_____

2. Reach agreement that a problem exists.
   Questions to use / consequences if problem continues:

_____

_____

_____

_____

_____

Figure 9.6

3. Discuss causes of the problem. Questions:

_____

_____

_____

_____

_____

_____

4. Discuss possible solutions and agree upon action(s).
   Identify specific action(s) to be taken.

_____

_____

_____

_____

_____

_____

_____

5. Document the session. How ?_____

_____

_____

_____

_____

_____

_____

_____

6. Follow-up on the session and recognize achievement or
   change. How ? When ?

_____

_____

_____

_____

_____

Figure 9.6 *(cont)*

1. Based on the facts of the situation, state the problem exactly and clearly. Use descriptive statements.
Prepare by writing down some of the descriptive statements you will use.

2. Reach agreement that a problem exists. Use questioning techniques/ identify consequences if problem continues.
Prepare by listing the questions you will use, the reasons why change is necessary and the possible consequences you will mention.

3. Discuss causes of the problem . Use questioning techniques.
Prepare for this step by listing some of the information questions you will use.

4. Discuss possible solutions and agree upon action(s). Identify the specific action(s) to be taken.
Prepare for this step by writing down descriptive statements and questions you will use. Make a note of some of the possible solutions and actions you might suggest.

5. Document the session.
The preparation form can be part of your documentation and attached to your memo on the session.

6. Follow-up on the coaching session.
Identify when you might follow-up and how you might recognize achievement or change.

Common situations

Situation: You are fairly new to the job and don't feel confident about coaching.
Response: Coaching is certainly more difficult when you're new to the job and are supervising people with more experience in the department or unit. Research shows that those employees who were chosen by the coach are more likely to be successfully coached than those who are already there when the coach assumed his or her position. Coming in from outside does

however bring with it certain advantages – you have no prior loyalties and may be able to see things more objectively. You need to observe the situation first, though, before you take any action. You need to collect information and be able to describe the situation before you can evaluate and act upon it.

Situation: The staff member argues with you and will not admit that his or her behaviour was wrong.
Response: If the person gets emotional or angry, ride out the storm. It won't help if you lose your temper too. Make sure you have presented the facts clearly using descriptive statements. Discuss the consequences if this situation or problem continues. Try to get across the idea that it's the person's problem and only he or she can resolve it. Again it's vital to get his or her agreement that a problem exists.

Situation: A staff member agrees with what you say but you feel he or she is not really committed to change.
Response: Discuss the consequences of not changing and the seriousness of the situation. Arrange for a follow-up meeting to check on progress.

Situation: A staff member is angry about company policies and regulations. He or she blames the policy and regulations for the problem you are discussing.
Response: Review the appropriate policies and regulations to ensure there is no misunderstanding. Discuss the reasons for these policies and regulations. Discuss the consequences of not following them. The person may be angry now, but he or she needs to think carefully about making any decisions that will vitally affect his or her future with the organization.

Situation: The staff member refuses to accept responsibility. He or she blames you for not providing enough support and other people for not doing their jobs properly.
Response: Use the coaching model to discuss the situation as a whole, including responsibilities. Try to see the situation from his or her perspective, then as objectively as possible. There may be some truth in what he or she says. If so, admit those parts which

seem to be true. Keep the focus, though, on what the staff member can do to prevent this problem from occurring again.

Action items

Use the Coaching Preparation Form, Figure 9.6, to prepare for a coaching session with one of your people.

CHAPTER 10

How to Conduct Effective Performance Reviews

> 'I'll be judge, I'll be jury,' said cunning old Fury; 'I'll try the whole cause, and condemn you to death'.
> Lewis Carroll, *Alice in Wonderland*.

Some managers and supervisors enjoy being judge and jury on their employees' work performance. They may not be able to condemn the employee to death but through performance review they have power over promotions, transfers, merit increases and sometimes whether an employee stays with the organization at all.

While some managers and supervisors don't worry about performance review, others feel unhappy and uncertain in their role as judge and jury. When they complete performance appraisal forms they worry about judging too subjectively and on the basis of too little evidence. They wonder how they can make the performance review discussion less emotionally charged – a constructive meeting rather than an ego-bruising affair dominated by arguments about past mistakes, salary increases and promotions.

The aim of this chapter is to help you to conduct constructive performance review sessions and work with employees to plan for the future. It should help you to make performance review a less stressful and more productive process for both you and your staff.

Your current situation

Think back to the last performance review meeting you con-

SELF-QUESTIONNAIRE ON PERFORMANCE REVIEW MEETINGS			
QUESTION	YES	NO	COMMENT
1. Did you feel uneasy about the performance review meeting with your employee?			
2. Did you adequately prepare, eg, complete an appraisal form, check back over records, etc.?			
3. Did the meeting take place in a good atmosphere?			
4. Did you discuss what your employee had achieved over the past year?			
5. Did you recognize his/her efforts over the past year?			
6. Did you discuss the employee's strengths?			
7. Did you discuss any improvements in the employee's performance?			
8. Did you make any plans or discuss assignments for next year?			
9. Did the meeting focus mainly on the past?			
10. Did the meeting focus mainly on the future?			
11. Did you feel satisfied at the end of the meeting?			
12. Do you think your employee felt satisfied?			
13. Did you learn valuable things from the meeting? If so, what?			

Figure 10.1

ducted. Then respond to the questions given in Figure 10.1. In the comments column add any details you think are important, eg, what preparations you made, what improvements were discussed.

Consider your responses and comments. What will you change for your next performance review meeting?

Why performance review is important

During the course of your day-to-day work, you are constantly giving advice and encouragement and working with your people to anticipate and resolve problems. Naturally, you give informal feedback on your people's performance. Pressure of time, however, and the lack of opportunity for discussion often limit the value of this informal feedback. In some situations employees have limited opportunities for uninterrupted conversation with their boss. A formal performance review is important then because it gives you an opportunity to meet separately with each member of staff and to take a detached and overall view of job performance and staff development. It encourages a systematic and regular joint stock-taking and planning for the future.

Performance review is potentially the most critical tool you can use to influence employees. There are two aspects of performance review – performance appraisal and performance planning. *Performance appraisal* judges the employee's work performance usually over the past year – it looks back to the past. *Performance planning* is concerned with improving an employee's performance and planning for future work – it looks to the future. Good performance reviews therefore, don't just summarize the past, they help determine future performance.

Systematic reviews are important to organizations for the following reasons.

● They require managers to communicate with their staff and discuss individual performance. Performance reviews can force managers to face up to problems of poor performance and attempt to deal with them.

● They provide justification for merit increases. As staff pay often includes an element for paying employees according to performance, it is important that the individual's contribution to the organization is fairly assessed.

● They identify employees' needs for support and training. When you meet with staff to review their past performance and determine future objectives, you can discuss areas where additional support or training would be helpful.

● They generate up-to-date information on the current skills and expertise of staff so that this might be used for manpower planning. Through performance review the organization is better equipped to match skills, career aspirations and experience with known or anticipated job slots.

Benefits of performance review

What's in it for you
Managers often give performance reviews a low priority because they see the problems involved in discussing job performance with employees, rather than the potential benefits of an effective performance review discussion. Systematic performance reviews can provide an opportunity for you to do the following.

● Get to know your staff better. A good manager or supervisor needs to be in touch with his or her staff. Through the performance review discussion you can demonstrate your concern for individuals and show that you notice the work your people do. As mentioned many times in this book, when people are 'noticed', this acts as a powerful motivator and can stimulate improved performance.

● Discuss and encourage improvements in individual performance. Good performance may not continue unless it's recognized, and the employee may lose the motivation to do well. If good performance *is* recognized, the employee may well become even better. Conversely, if unsatisfactory performance is ignored it will continue or often become worse. Generally people see no reason to change their behaviour if it appears acceptable to their manager and the organization.

● Discuss new tasks and targets. With each member of your staff in turn you can stand back from the day-to-day workload and discuss goals and appropriate plans for the future.

● Help you to identify individual training and development needs. Through the performance review process you can learn what support or training an employee might need to accomplish job targets and improve his or her performance.

● Evaluate a person's suitability for other responsibilities and assignments, including promotion. When you discuss future work plans you can talk more generally about the staff member's career, skills and ambitions.

● Gain more experience in manpower planning and in making difficult personnel decisions. Learning to conduct professional performance reviews can help prepare you for increased responsibility.

What's in it for the employee
Systematic performance reviews can achieve the following.

● Clarify job requirements and future tasks and targets. In this way performance review sessions can be particularly helpful to individuals in the first few years of their career or in a new job.

● Provide a channel for feedback. Many performance problems occur and continue because of lack of feedback. Through the performance review the employee gains more information on the manager's expectations and views on his or her job performance. Performance review should not be a one-way process and the employee can also express his or her concerns and aspirations.

● Motivate employees to achieve more. Performance review sessions should provide recognition of employees' work and efforts and let people know how they are succeeding in their jobs.

● Give the employee time and space to vent his or her concerns and frustrations. If the meeting is conducted in a relaxed atmosphere and the manager takes a sympathetic and constructive approach, the employee will feel relieved and pleased that he or she has been listened to.

● Lead to more support from the manager and training and development opportunities.

Given the above benefits, performance review *seems* a good thing. But in the *real* world there are still problems and performance reviews will never be easy or free from difficulties. A great amount of effort has gone into the development of better systems and performance review forms. The success of any system or form, however, depends upon the attitudes, knowledge and skills of the people using it. The bottom line is that you must learn to use your own review process in the most constructive way.

Performance review guidelines

One of the most popular and effective approaches to performance review is the Three Form approach. Here the employee completes a self-appraisal, the supervisor completes his own appraisal of the employee and the final appraisal is a product of both viewpoints. An outline of this approach is shown in the Guidelines, Figure 10.2, and described in the notes below.

Preparation

1. Establish date and time for discussion.
Too often performance appraisals are left until the last minute and then done in a hurried manner. The results are poor with managers feeling guilty and employees feeling unimportant and

PERFORMANCE REVIEW GUIDELINES

PREPARATION

1. ESTABLISH DATE AND TIME FOR DISCUSSION ☐
2. HAVE EMPLOYEE COMPLETE SELF-APPRAISAL ☐
3. GATHER INFORMATION ON EMPLOYEE'S
   PERFORMANCE ☐
4. DRAFT PERFORMANCE REVIEW FORM ☐
5. DISCUSS REVIEW WITH YOUR BOSS ☐

CONDUCTING THE DISCUSSION

1. PREPARE FOR DISCUSSION ☐
2. ESTABLISH CONSTRUCTIVE CLIMATE AND TWO-WAY
   CONVERSATION ☐
3. SHARE YOUR ASSESSMENT OF EMPLOYEE
   PERFORMANCE ☐
4. DISCUSS AREAS FOR IMPROVEMENT ☐
5. PLAN FOR NEXT YEAR
6. SUMMARIZE AND CLOSE DISCUSSION ON A
   POSITIVE NOTE ☐

FOLLOW-UP
☐
1. DOCUMENT DISCUSSION ☐
2. FOLLOW UP ON ANY AGREEMENTS AND ACTIONS

Figure 10.2

let down. Give the employee at least a week's notice and preparation time before the performance review discussion. Check your own calendar and with the employee identify a time when you will both be free. Allow enough time for the discussion. It is unlikely that a performance review discussion can be conducted in less than 45 minutes. This may seem a fairly long time but it's a small investment for what is a critical part of your job.

2. Have employee complete a self-appraisal.
When you arrange for the discussion, ask the person to complete the same performance review form that you will complete. This ensures that the employee takes time to think about his or her performance and future development in a comprehensive and structured way. Ask the employee to hand in a copy of the completed form a few days before the discussion so that you can take it into consideration when you complete your own form. In preparation for the meeting, you might also ask the employee to consider:

- the past, in terms of main achievements, problems and their causes, what he or she enjoyed, what he or she did not enjoy;
- the present, in terms of the person's current workload, strengths and areas for improvement;
- the future, in terms of where the department is going, the employee's own aims, what help or training is needed and any other points.

When the employee hands in the self-appraisal you might discuss and clarify some of the points made so that both you and the employee have as full a picture as possible.

3. Gather information on employee's performance.
As employee performance *in the current job* is the key issue, look at the job description, job requirements and the established goals or standards. Look back at the previous year's performance review records and identify the objectives and targets that were established then. How has the employee performed in achieving

those targets? Check your records (activity reports, project reports) and memory against the information in the employee's self-appraisal.

Some jobs, however, offer more easily identifiable objectives or targets than others: for example, project-based jobs compared with maintenance jobs. In addition, most people have to take on responsibilities and tasks that have nothing to do with their annual objectives or targets. How a person behaves in dealing with all these additional tasks and responsibilities is important and to assess these factors you need to consider the person's overall performance over the past year.

One way to do this is to identify three or four critical incidents or events that you remember occurring during the year. Then consider the following questions:

- How did the person behave during these incidents?
- How did you judge him or her at the time?
- How did other staff judge him or her?
- Did the incident reflect well on the employee's job performance?
- How did the incident reflect on the department?

You might list a few of the words or phrases which come to mind as you consider these incidents and answer the questions. For example:

- professional approach;
- took the initiative;
- overlooked important details;
- helped out colleagues;
- impatient with others;
- persistent in making sure the job was done.

Finally, if the employee's job involves a lot of contact with other supervisors, clients and customers, you might collect their views and opinions on the employee's performance.

4. Draft performance review form.
When a manager makes general and judgemental comments, the

DESCRIBING PERFORMANCE

Think of the people you conduct performance reviews on. Change the following vague general statements into more specific descriptions of their performance. Use the names of people in your department. For example:

General: Employee is highly reliable and always does a good job.

More specific: *Jean* always completes assignments on time. When two key staff were absent she took on additional responsibilities.

1. General: Employee's quality of work is excellent.

   More specific: _____

   _____

2. General: Employee gets through a lot of work in the department.

   More specific: _____

   _____

3. General: Employee's safety performance is normal.

   More specific: _____

4. General: Employee communicates well generally but needs to improve in some areas.

   More specific: _____

5. General: Employee's performance is very unsatisfactory.

   More specific: _____

6. General: Employee helps to train and develop other staff.

   More specific: _____

Figure 10.3

employee often sees this as an attack and becomes defensive. As you complete the review form, therefore, use descriptive statements to write about performance in each of the review areas. You need to be specific in your description so that there can be a reasonable discussion of strengths and weaknesses and plans for improvement. To give you some practice in changing general and judgemental comments into descriptive statements, you might complete the exercise given in Figure 10.3.

When you complete a performance review form you might pair a general statement with a specific statement (like the example given in Figure 10.3). In this way, the specific statement serves as critical evidence, or as an example to support the general statement.

When you have completed the review form, read it through to

DESCRIBING PERFORMANCE – SOME SPECIFIC STATEMENTS

Here are some examples of more specific performance statements:

1. Employee has high standards and works to ensure that assignments are always professional with very few errors.
2. Employee completed three planned major projects this year. In addition he (or she) completed an unplanned inspection project.
3. No accidents during the past year. Employee follows the safety guidelines.
4. Communicates well with clients over the phone. Some improvement required in report writing.
5. Regularly fails to meet the deadlines for completion of monthly record keeping assignments. Requires close supervision and follow-up.
6. Has trained Michael and Joan on how to produce reports on the computer.

Figure 10.4

PERFORMANCE REVIEW - COMMON ERRORS

Below is a list of common errors made in completing performance review forms.
- How many of these errors might occur when you appraise your staff?
- Consider each error carefully in terms of your most recent performance reviews.

Indicate with a check mark (✔) whether you have a problem or not with each of these errors.

ERROR	DESCRIPTION	NOT A PROBLEM	PROBLEM
Just like me	Using personal standards as your reference point. Appraising someone more favourably because they seem like you.		
Compliance	Giving higher ratings to those employees who always agree or always give way to you, and lower ratings to more assertive staff.		
Recency	Being over-influenced by recent events, either favourably or unfavourably.		
Halo effect	Appraising someone high in all aspects of the job because of one outstanding characteristic.		
Horns effect	Appraising somone low in all aspects of the job because of one characteristic you strongly dislike.		
Spillover	Allowing past appraisals of this person to influence the current appraisal.		
Proximity	Appraising similarly those items next to each other on the review form.		
Central tendency	Avoiding the high / low scores on a rating scale and concentrating on the middle scores.		
Avoidance	Avoiding negative comments because of likely difficulties when you discuss them with your own boss or with the employee in the review discussion.		

Now you have identified which errors are a problem for you, look at your current performance appraisal forms. How can they be improved?

Figure 10.5

ensure that it gives a balanced view of the employee's strengths and weaknesses.

Performance review – common errors
Figure 10.5 contains a list of common errors made in completing performance review forms. How many of these errors might occur when you appraise your staff? Consider each error carefully in terms of your most recent performance reviews. Indicate with a tick whether you have a problem or not with each of these errors.

Now you have identified which errors are a problem for you, look at your current performance appraisal forms. How can they be improved?

5. Discuss your review with your boss.
In many organizations, the employee's performance review form is completed by the supervisor and then discussed with his or her supervisor at the next level. When you meet with your boss, listen to his or her views on your people's performance rather than focusing on justifying your own comments and ratings. Your boss may have information that you do not have and will often provide a different perspective on people's performance. Don't be a pushover though – if you've done your preparation properly and can support your judgements with objective evidence then you owe it to your people to defend your assessments.

Conducting the discussion

1. Prepare for the discussion.
The most important feature of the performance review discussion is the atmosphere in which it is conducted. Make sure you hold the meeting in private to avoid interruptions or anyone overhearing. Prepare yourself mentally by focusing on what you want to achieve – a discussion that:

- demonstrates your recognition of the person's achievements;
- recognizes that the person has detailed experience of the job and potentially useful ideas for improvement;

- involves joint exploration of any performance problems;
- generates mutual feedback;
- focuses on future performance rather than arguing about the past.

2. Establish constructive climate and two-way conversation.
When the employee enters, welcome him or her and outline the purpose of the discussion. At all costs avoid giving the impression that performance review is a meaningless chore which needs to be completed only for the purposes of satisfying personnel or 'those upstairs'. This kind of 'buck-passing' only indicates a manager's weakness.

You might open the discussion on a positive friendly note by highlighting one of the employee's recent achievements and discussing it first. Then have the employee review performance over the past twelve months. He or she might do this by referring to the review form they completed. This approach enables the employee to select where to begin and can lead to a relatively candid assessment of actual performance. While the employee is talking, you should be an interested listener but you might ask clarifying questions and make notes (making notes not only provides a record but shows a genuine interest and respect for what the employee is saying). At this point you can learn more from listening than from talking and you have a rare opportunity to find out what the employee feels about his or her work and your management.

When the employee has completed this review, discuss the information and clarify any points by asking for more detail. If there's a space on the form for areas for improvement and the employee has left it blank, ask him or her how it might be completed. If the employee has listed strengths, has he or she listed any weaknesses? The aim here is to get the employee to look as objectively as possible at his or her performance and to look for and agree to improvements.

3. Share your assessment of employee performance over the past year.
Now you might refer to the form you have completed and any other notes. Discuss the employee's achievements and strengths

in detail to show that you recognize his or her distinctive contribution and so that you can build on these strengths. Whenever possible, refer back to the form the employee completed and indicate any similarities, or points where you think the employee did not give himself or herself sufficient credit. Don't be tempted to rush through the 'achievements' and 'strengths' in order to get to the 'improvements'. By focusing mainly on 'improvements' you may be distorting the picture and failing to give sufficient credit where it's due.

4. Discuss areas for improvement.

The most difficult part of any performance review is discussing unsatisfactory performance and areas for improvement. Generally, the most effective remedy for poor performance is to focus on the future rather than on the past. Focusing on the past is often unproductive for two reasons: first, there is no way that the mistakes of the past can be undone, and second, discussions that focus totally on the past are likely to lead to arguments due to the manager and the employee having different perceptions of past events. People can learn from past mistakes but the lessons are more acceptable if the emphasis is on what the employee will do differently from now on, rather than on these past mistakes.

Employees who work in a non-threatening and constructive atmosphere are more likely to discuss their shortcomings or areas for improvement during the performance review discussion. When this occurs you can be supportive by saying something like, 'It's good that you've recognized that. What can we do to improve the situation?'

If the employee doesn't identify the area of weak performance, you must do so. One way to approach this is to describe the impact of the poor performance on the organization and other members of the work team. Another is to review job expectations and standards. If the employee is unaware or unsure about these expectations and standards, you must make them clear.

You need to discuss any differences between what you expected and what the employee achieved – you need to discuss what these differences are and why they occurred. Discussion here needs to be a joint problem-solving session and you should be prepared to consider your own responsibility for any inadequacies in job performance. The focus here, though, should not be on past problems but on ensuring that differences between expectations and achievements are less in future.

In this discussion you should:

- Use descriptive statements and questions like:
  'We are a month behind on this project, Frank. Can you tell me why and what we can do to catch up?'
  'Three people in your unit resigned last month, Jean. Can you tell me about that?'
  'Your report was a week late, Malcolm. How can we improve this situation?'
- Be supportive, not authoritarian. Compare these two statements:
  Authoritarian: 'This is what you should do to meet the deadline in future'.
  Supportive: 'What do you think we should do to meet the deadline in future?'
- Be flexible, not dogmatic. Compare these two statements:
  Dogmatic: 'This is the best solution – this is what you should do'.
  Flexible: 'This seems to me the best solution. What do you think?'

With some people – for example an experienced and mature professional – a verbal discussion on how to improve a specific aspect of performance may be enough. With less experienced or mature staff a more formal approach might be more helpful. A simple agreement like the one given in Figure 10.6 might be used.

At the end of this discussion you must make it clear that, although you recognize and have listened to the employee's views, you must evaluate performance yourself. In cases of disagreement, the manager or supervisor must prevail.

5. Plan for next year.
Explain the department's goals and objectives for the next twelve months. At this stage it may be best just to discuss the individual's

---

PERSONAL PERFORMANCE IMPROVEMENT ACTION PLAN

Manager/Supervisor: _____

Staff Member: _____ Date: _____

PROBLEM. Write down the problem you and the employee have identified. For example: Need to increase my skills in dealing with customers.

ACTION. Look at the options – off-the-job training, on-the-job training, job rotation, coaching, mentoring, self-managed learning, etc. Include your own involvement and actions as well as the employee's. Give dates for the action if possible. For example:

- Attend the customer relations course – September 11.
- Discuss the course with manager – September 15.
- Work on assignment with J. Martin, an experienced staff member – October/November.
- Make a joint report and presentation on the assignment to the manager and other staff members – December.

REVIEW. When, who with, what? For example: After the joint presentation in December, meet with the manager to discuss performance.

Figure 10.6

potential tasks and targets in a general way. You don't want to 'overload' this performance review meeting and more detailed discussion of future work is often best left to another meeting. This kind of goal-setting meeting at the beginning of a performance period is described in Chapter 1.

The general planning discussion may, however, provide an opportunity for widening the conversation and linking work requirements with the employee's personal development. You

might discuss what training and development needs and opportunities will arise from future work goals and find out the
employee's thoughts on his or her own training needs. You
should also explore the employee's views and feelings about
longer-term development, transfers, promotion and career
progression.

In this discussion the emphasis should be on why and in what
way the person needs to be trained or developed. Avoid
discussing possible courses as if the training catalogue were a
shopping list, but don't ignore off-the job training (see Chapter 6)
and also discuss alternative methods of learning to formal
training courses.

During this planning discussion you might use a Task and
Target Sheet like the one shown in Chapter 1, Figure 1.2.

6. Summarize and close the discussion on a positive note.
Many performance reviews fail because the manager and the
employee end the session with different views about what
happened and what was agreed upon. Summarize what has been
discussed and agreed. Reinforce the praise for good work. Review
and show enthusiasm and confidence in the action plans that
have been agreed upon and end on a positive note.

Follow-up

1. Document discussion.
Complete the final review form, making any changes or additional comments that you think necessary as a result of your
discussion. Add a summary of your discussion and give the forms
to the employee for signature and, if necessary, for him or her to
make a copy.

2. Follow up on any agreements and actions.
Without coaching and follow-up your performance review
process will be limited in its effectiveness. A survey carried out at
Motorola Semi-conductors in 1982 showed that with 80 managers appraising over 500 staff, 80 per cent of performance
problems identified required the coaching support of the apprais-

ing manager for their solution. Only 20 per cent required formal training. Coaching, therefore, is a key management skill and the link between recognition of poor performance and performance improvement (see Chapter 9, How to Coach your People).

Ensure that any training or development activities that were agreed upon are planned for and actually happen during the next year.

Common situations

Situation: Upper management puts pressure on you to lower your performance review ratings.
Response: Look at your ratings as objectively as possible. There is a natural upward bias in ratings as managers try to:

- Improve morale in their own departments.
- Make sure their people receive as much money as possible from the limited amount available for merit increases.
- Record and reward performance improvements. For example, you might want to encourage an employee who performed poorly at the beginning of the year but who has improved.
- Avoid confrontations with some employees.

If your organization's performance review system is to retain any integrity it must be monitored so that over-raters and under-raters become aware of and correct their bias. To protect your appraisals and your own credibility make sure that your ratings are justified in terms of specific performances. If you make only vague general comments on the review forms you are vulnerable to having your ratings lowered. You will lose credibility and your staff will lose recognition, opportunities for development and deserved merit increases.

Situation: You have asked your staff to complete performance appraisal forms but one of your employees won't complete the sections of the form that deal with performance improvements. He or she says 'That's up to you'.
Response: You need to get the employee's commitment to improvement and the best way to do that is through his or her

involvement in identifying areas that could be improved. Point out to the employee that improvement in performance is everyone's responsibility. *You* can't improve someone's performance – it's up to the individual. A first step is for the employee to recognize the need for change and to try to identify areas for improvement.

Situation: One of your people is a constant problem. His performance is unsatisfactory. The same problems have been discussed at performance reviews over the years and he's been given additional training, yet there is very little improvement.
Response: A lot of time and effort is often spent in trying to 'develop' marginal employees and bring them up to standard. In many cases this means that management resources are expended on the wrong people. The people with potential who are going to provide a return to the organization for its investment in staff development and training may be neglected. If you tell most managers that they have made a bad investment with respect to capital outlay, they quickly realize it is not a good idea to throw good money after bad. Yet a lot of time and energy are spent in working with the wrong people – those who do not meet the required performance standards.

In some situations it's a fallacy to believe that the method of approach makes a significant difference. In many cases it is doubtful that anything will remedy the situation other than removing the person from the particular job.

Situation: The employee begins to criticize you and your job performance.
Response: Most of the advice and suggestions given in this chapter are designed to prevent you and the employee getting into a situation where you criticize each other in a destructive way. When you find yourself being criticized, keep calm and think. Avoid an immediate emotional reaction. If necessary, pause and take a deep breath. DO NOT:

- Deny the criticism.
- Defend or try to justify yourself.

- Begin to argue.
- Run away from the situation.
- Say 'Yes but . . .'.

Instead you might follow this three-step approach to dealing with criticism:

- Listen to the critic and repeat back the criticism. When the employee hears the criticism repeated, he or she may feel this is too strong and that they have reacted emotionally. The criticism may be retracted or modified.
- Ask the critic to specify the problem or give specific examples. Keep asking questions until you understand the critic's point of view and feelings.
- Offer or ask for a solution to the problem. For example, 'If I did XYZ, would that solve the problem?' You and the critic might then agree on a solution.

Situation: The employee asks about opportunities for promotion. He or she has worked in the department for a long time and has seen others promoted.
Response. Ask the employee why he or she thinks they should be promoted. Then ask questions to clarify any information points and the person's feelings. Promotion usually depends upon a variety of factors, only some of which are under the employee's and manager's control. The employee may be qualified but the situation in the organization or department may mean that there are no promotion 'slots'. If promotion is unlikely in the near future, you might discuss new assignments with the employee. These may increase his or her potential for promotion and enrich the current job.

Action items

List three things you will do to improve your own performance in conducting performance reviews.

1.

2.

3.

APPENDIX
How to Develop and Use Training or Presentation Aids

Here are some guidelines and suggestions for developing and using the most common training and presentation aids:

1. Handouts
2. Flipcharts
3. Overhead transparencies
4. Slides
5. Video

1. Handouts

Handouts can be used in the following ways.

• To reinforce what you say. You might provide a training outline for employees to note down points or questions and use either for discussion or future reference. By using an outline, employees avoid having to spend a lot of time copying down notes.

• To explain and organize a group activity. Employees can follow the instructions and steps given in the handout.

• To assess learning. You can provide a question sheet, for example after a video, to test how much employees have learned and how they might apply the new information. Your first questions might test their memory and understanding of the material but your last one might ask them how they might use it on the job. This last question would pull everything together and provide for a practical discussion.

Preparing handouts

1. Give clear simple instructions or ask questions with short sentences. Test out these instructions or questions by having someone else read them for possible confusion or ambiguity.

2. Consider using a mix of 'closed' questions and rather general 'open' questions. The closed questions require employees to retrieve detailed information – for example, from a manual, film, video or other resource. The open questions require them to express their own ideas and opinions and encourage thought and discussion in a training session.

3. Provide one or two questions which oblige employees to select relevant information and apply it to their job situations.

4. Try to limit your handout to one page. That will make it easier for employees to refer to and use.

5. Test the handout several times before using it. Which instructions or questions are not clear? Which questions do employees need more space for answering? Do they need more explanation or guidance on a particular task?

6. Plan how you will discuss employees' responses to the handout. Predict possible answers for your questions. That way you can check on any confusion in the questions, avoid duplication (questions that lead to the same answers) and prepare yourself for a variety of responses.

2. Flipcharts

The blackboard always evokes memories of school. The flipchart, however, is identified with business and industry and reinforces an adult meeting atmosphere. Flipcharts are particularly effective with small audiences because they have an informal appearance that invites interruptions and interaction between the audience and the speaker.

Another advantage of the flipchart is flexibility. Prepared pages or flipcharts can be brought to the session. The advantages of prepared pages are that you can:

- Produce neat and legible printing.
- Save time in the training session or presentation by not having to write up these pages.
- Use the pages as guidelines or notes for yourself.

A prepared flipchart or pages can be used in conjunction with 'ad lib' pages or flipcharts that you produce during the session. The prepared pages might be used to show the title of the training session or presentation, the objectives, the agenda, instructions for a specific task, models, steps or other material that you know you will use. Obviously, these prepared pages can be used again in later training sessions or presentations.

The 'ad lib' pages or flipchart can be used to record responses that you obtain from people, group work reports or other feedback information. Compared to alternative media, the flipchart is easily portable and you can roll up your prepared flipcharts and use them away from your usual work site.

Preparing the flipchart

1. Decide what pages you want to prepare in advance and which pages you will produce as a result of discussion or group activities. Draft your prepared pages on sheets of paper or cards before you actually begin work on the flipchart.

2. Lay the flipchart on a flat surface so that you can work easily with it. If possible, use water-soluble markers – permanent markers often bleed through onto the next page.

3. On each page write down only the main points and limit these to no more than five or six. Abbreviate any long words or

sentences. You can explain and add more detail when you refer to these points in your training session.

4. Leave a blank page between each page you write. Flipchart pages tend to be thin and can be read through. When you are referring to one page you don't want your audience to be reading the next one.

5. Give each page a printed heading and write clearly with letters at least two inches high. Most people's writing tends to be too small. Leave about one and a half inches between key points. Lightly squared flipchart pages can help with this but if these are unavailable, use a ruler and pencil to make guidelines. Then, after you've printed your information, erase the guidelines.

6. Use two or three colours for variety and to emphasize key points or key words. The page heading should be a different colour from the points.

7. If you expect to refer to a flipchart page more than once, mark it with a paper clip or a sticker.

8. Fix the flipchart on a flipchart stand. Check the stand for stability and go through the pages as you will during the training session or presentation. Check that the pages are in the correct sequence and that there there is nothing more you need to add.

9. If you are travelling with prepared flipchart pages, tear them off the pad, roll them up and place them in a cardboard tube.

Using the flipchart

When you use the flipchart:

1. Stand at the side as you speak and write so that you can maintain eye contact with employees. Avoid talking to the board as you write things down.

2. Make sure your audience can see what you write. Don't use small writing and small diagrams.

3. Make sure each new page has a printed heading. This improves the appearance of your pages and makes it easier to review later.

4. Record only the main ideas. Limit the number of points on a page to no more than five or six and do not fill a page to the bottom. People at the back of the room may not be able to see.

5. Use a pointer to indicate important ideas, then turn to the audience and speak.

6. Pause after you complete a page. Before you turn to a new page, allow time for participants to read and, if necessary, make notes.

7. Let employees use flipchart pages to record the results of their group work. This makes it easier for the results to be discussed afterwards.

8. Tear off pages and tape them up on the wall for easy reference later in the session.

9. Turn to a blank sheet or the cover page when you finish. Flipchart pages showing from a previous activity can distract people from a new one.

3. Overhead transparencies

Overhead transparencies (OHTs) are more formal than the flipchart and work well with audiences of small to moderate size. Using OHTs helps your planning and leads to more organized and effective training sessions and presentations. You seem better prepared, more professional, more persuasive and more in control. There is a tendency, therefore, for audiences to accept your ideas or plans and for favourable decisions to be reached.

Preparing your OHTs early helps you with your outlining and to focus on the main points. The main content of your training session appears on the OHTs and you can use them over and over again and ensure a consistent presentation.

Preparing overhead transparencies

1. When you outline your training session indicate important points where you might use OHTs.

2. Draft your OHTs on sheets of paper or cards. For each transparency decide what the message is and what the key ideas and words are. Try to express this *one idea or message* in a maximum of six lines with no more than six words a line. More information and words than this can lead to confusion and the loss of the central message. Remember the KISS principle – Keep It Short and Simple. Don't treat OHTs like pages in a book and fill the screen with information and small print.

3. Use key words and phrases rather than sentences, but preserve grammatical consistency if possible. The points should all begin with the same part of speech – action verbs or nouns, etc.

4. Choose a clear and consistent design for your transparencies and concentrate information in the centre. Most screens are horizontal so use a horizontal format to allow full use of the screen and make it easier to project over the heads of participants. Avoid vertical lettering on your OHTs as it is difficult to read.

5. Leave a three-quarter inch margin for the frame. Letters should be at least one inch high for good legibility with half an inch between lines. Rule lines in pencil to keep your letters the same size and on a line, then erase the pencil lines afterwards.

6. Direct attention to the key ideas by using colour, boxing or underlining. Be consistent and use the same colours for headings, numbering, etc.

7. Use bullets (●) rather than numbers when you are listing items that are not sequential, eg the features of a project.

8. Do not reproduce a printed page on a transparency. The diagram or writing will be too small.

9. Use overlays – one or more additional transparencies placed on top of the original one – when you want to show the stages in a project or process. Each additional transparency builds upon the previous ones until the entire visual process is complete. Taping overlays to a cardboard frame can ensure sharp alignment of transparencies during a training session or presentation.

Producing transparencies
If you do not have graphics professionals or access to computer graphics, you can produce your own OHTs in the following way.

1. Produce the graphic on A4 paper.

2. Avoid type and use a lettering system. Use outline letters and colour these in later with permanent overhead projector pens. Use colour as much as possible.

3. Photocopy the graphic onto transparency film with a normal copier, or photocopy onto paper and then use a thermofax copier.

4. Mount the OHTs in cardboard frames. These frames make useful places to put your notes – either on the frame itself or on a sticker – and can help guide you through the presentation. These notes will be particularly useful if this is the first time you have made the presentation. Frames also make transparencies easier to transport and store.

5. Number your OHTs so that if they are knocked on the floor or mixed up, you can sort them out. If you are undecided on the order or may change it, number the transparencies in pencil or use easily removed labels.

6. Analyse your OHTs and see if any can be eliminated. Some transparencies might be optional – eliminated if it's necessary to shorten the session, or included if it's necessary to give further explanation or lengthen the session. Dealing with transparencies in this way gives you more flexibility.

7. Decide whether you want the audience to copy down points from the transparencies or whether you will provide print copies of the OHTs at the end. The latter is more professional – it provides a reference or record, saves time and prevents interruptions when those people who want to make notes ask you to keep a transparency on the screen.

8. Practise using the transparencies before your actual training session and try to ensure a smooth link between your narrative and your OHTs.

9. Make sure the projector lens and the projection surface are clean before you start.

10. To ensure that your transparencies don't project crookedly, tape a straight-edged piece of cardboard along the top edge of the projector surface. Then slide each new transparency against the straight edge.

11. Make sure your projector works well and a spare projector or bulb is available. When you're setting-up the room for your training session, use your first transparency, walk to the back of the room and view the transparency as a member of the audience – check it for clarity, screen placement and image distortion.

Using overhead transparencies

1. Provide print copies of transparencies. If employees don't have to copy your points, they can focus on listening to you and understanding the information.

2. Use the projector with the room lights on. You might dim the

lights but don't distract people by constantly switching them on and off.

3. Stand at the side. Avoid getting between the overhead projector and the screen or blocking the employees' view.

4. Mask information. Control the pace and give a sense of movement to your presentation by masking parts of transparencies with a piece of card or paper. The masking card or piece of paper should be placed *beneath* the transparency and then slid down – if you put the mask on top of the transparency, you will need to hold it there to prevent it dropping off.

Use the mask to gradually reveal each point as you deal with it so that the visual and verbal focus is on one point at a time. This is particularly important when you have lists of points. If your audience can see all the points, they may be reading Point 6 when you are talking about Point 1. Employees may also spend time copying things down and miss your comments. Through masking you can avoid this and link the transparency directly with your narrative.

5. Do not use use so many OHTs that the projector becomes a reading machine. Overhead transparencies are a visual medium.

6. Use a pointer and point at the transparency, *not at the screen*. Pointing at the screen casts shadows and takes you away from the audience. You can leave the pointer or pen on the transparency pointing to something on the screen while you talk about it.

7. Do not flip transparencies on and off. Give employees time to absorb the material and make any notes.

8. Use the on/off switch effectively. When you want the audience to focus on a transparency, switch on. When you want them to focus on you and what you are saying, switch off. In particular, do not leave the projector switched on for a long time without a transparency in place. This distracts attention from what you are saying or doing.

9. Increase group involvement. Elicit information or ideas from employees and use water-soluble transparency markers to write them on a blank transparency.

4. Slides

Slides tend to be more formal and authoritative than the flipchart or OHTs and are often used for business or project briefings to management audiences. Slides generally discourage participation and interaction because of their formal appearance and because the lighting is dimmed. Slide presentations tend to be too formal to use in training sessions and are most appropriate for presentations to medium- and large-size audiences.

Preparing slides

1. Complete a small index card for each slide. Describe what appears on the slide and indicate any production notes, such as whether the slide should be a long shot or close up. On the other side of the card write down what you plan to say when you present the slide. After completing all the cards, put them into sequence. You can move, add or delete cards to complete your presentation. Once they are numbered, the cards become your 'shooting script'.

2. Use photographs, diagrams, charts, graphs or flowcharts. A slide presentation needs to be visual and there should be a variety of images. If you have only words to show, it may be better to use overhead transparencies rather than slides.

3. Vary the pace of your presentation. Provide some slides – for example, charts and graphs – which you will spend time on and discuss. These can be supported by photographs or illustrations which you might move through quickly.

4. Condense any verbal information on the slides into not more than six lines and six words per line. Keep the words on the slides horizontal, especially on charts.

5. Use a consistent design for your series of slides and follow the same design rules as for OHTs. You might use several colours in your diagrams or charts but for the background it's best to use just one colour.

Using slides
The following points will help you conduct a presentation using slides. Before you start:

1. Check the focus and picture size on the screen. The greater the distance between the projector and the screen, the larger the picture.

2. Rehearse to check that each slide in the carousel is in the correct sequence and the right way up. Each slide should have a number on a sticker in the top right hand corner.

When you start:

1. Introduce the slide programme. You might make the session more interactive by inviting the audience to look at particular items for discussion afterwards.

2. Sound interested and enthusiastic to overcome any passive TV-watching atmosphere.

3. Use the remote control and stand well away from the projector.

4. Expand upon what is on the screen but don't read too much text from the slides – this is irritating when people can read themselves.

5. Be prepared to move back to particular slides during the question and answer session.

5. Video

Every year *Training* magazine conducts a survey of training and development in American companies; since 1987 video has been the most popular medium in company training. Major reasons for video's popularity are its convenience and ease of use. Compared with film, video is easier to stop and start and therefore comment on; it also tends to be easier to use (just load the cassette) and more hardy. Another factor in this growing popularity has been the rapid increase in the number of videos produced for training and development purposes.

Showing a video by itself, however, is not training. You need to pay attention to selecting an appropriate video – one which fits your objectives and your employees and can be integrated with other activities in your training session.

Selecting video

The video assessment report, Figure A.1, can be used in order to select videos. The following notes explain how the report might be used.

Purpose(s) of assessment.
Note down why you are looking at the video – the training session(s) for which you are interested in using it.

Video title
Write down the title.

Running time.
More than 20 minutes without a stop or pause point usually bores people. You also need the timing for your agenda or session plan.

Cost.
Note the rental and purchase costs. Will you use this video enough times to justify purchase?

Session topic.
Identify the topic of your training session.

Session objective(s).
Writing down your objectives will help you to focus on how closely the video fits them.

Useful training points.
Here you might note the main ideas covered in the video, points you might focus on in the activity following the programme, or quite simply anything you find it useful to make a note of.

Advantages of using this video.
Listing these will help with any justification required and help you make up your own mind as to the value of using the programme.

Disadvantages of using this video.
Identify any problems or confusions that might arise.

How to overcome disadvantages.
How might you introduce the video to prevent problems or confusion arising? Perhaps you could stop or pause the video at any difficult or potentially confusing points and then explain.

Cost justification (based on number of participants or importance of training).
Programme cost per participant is a good measure, but you also need to consider other factors such as the number of times the video may be used and the relative importance of the training session.

Fits in with session objective(s).
Video purely for the sake of variety is a mistake. A video may be very interesting but if it doeṣn't support your objectives, it can distract employees from the message you're trying to convey.

Fits employees' knowledge and skill levels.
A video that seems basic will 'turn off' employees. Conversely, a video which assumes a slightly higher knowledge or skill level than the employees possess may flatter them and often prove successful.

VIDEO ASSESSMENT REPORT

Purpose(s) of assessment:_____
_____

Video title:_____
Running time:_____   Cost:_____
Session topic: _____
_____

Session objective(s): _____
_____
_____
_____
_____

Useful training points:_____
_____
_____
_____
_____

Advantages of using this video: _____
_____
_____
_____

Disadvantages of using this video: _____
_____
_____

How to overcome disadvantages: _____
_____
_____

Cost justification (based on number of participants or
importance of training):_____
_____
_____

Figure A.1

VIDEO ASSESSMENT REPORT

VIDEO FEATURES

	YES	NO
Fits in with session objective(s)		
Fits employees' knowledge and skill levels		
Gains and maintains employee interest		
Provides appropriate content and examples		
Uses appropriate language - minimal jargon		
Provides up-to-date information		
Is segmented with stop or pause points		
Is supported by a trainer guide		
Is supported by exercises or activities		
Is satisfactory in terms of technical quality		
Fits the type of playback equipment available		

Figure A.1 *(cont)*

Gains and maintains employee interest.
The first few minutes of the video are critical. Employees need to listen actively, not just enjoy the cinema or watch TV.

Provides appropriate content and examples.
Check that the programme presents characters and situations which your employees can relate to. A group of professionals are not likely to be influenced if the characters in a video are clerical staff. A group of British salesmen are not likely to be influenced if the video characters are women working in the USA.

Uses appropriate language with minimal jargon.
Put yourself in the place of your audience. Is there too much jargon for them? Does the video speak down to them or could it be considered infantile? American programmes often use cartoon characters but British professionals tend to react with hostility to the cartoon approach.

Provides up-to-date information.
If the programme seems old-fashioned and out-of-date, this tends to make you and your training seem old-fashioned and out-of-date.

Is segmented with stop or pause points.
These points will enable you to make the session more interactive and give you more control over the training material.

Is supported by a trainer guide.
A guide saves time and often provides some useful suggestions for activities.

Is supported by exercises or activities.
Again, this will save time. Even if you don't use these materials as they stand, you might adapt them for your own specific purposes.

Is satisfactory in terms of technical quality.
Even minor faults can result in major distractions. Don't risk using a poor quality programme.

Fits the type of playback equipment available.
You need to check that you have the necessary playback equipment available. Video programmes come in a variety of formats – VHS, Beta, ¾ inch, 1 inch, U-Matic. There are also a variety of standards with NTSC being the American standard and PAL/SECAM being the standard in Britain and Europe. These formats and standards are not interchangeable so you need to check that the video is compatible with the equipment available.

The two blank rows on the video assessment report (Figure A.1) enable you to add any additional features you want to assess.

Preparing to show video

1. Once you have selected a video, preview it once more to become familiar with the parts you plan to use. Make notes while you watch so that you can explain complex topics and develop support materials. Notes will make you familiar enough with the video to discuss it with employees and also help you prepare oral or written questions to guide a discussion.

2. If you intend to use only part of a video or to stop at certain points, make a note of the counter numbers where you plan to stop and restart the programme.

3. Plan activities to accompany the video. These may range from informal discussion, a questionnaire on the programme content or application exercises in which employees use what they learned from the video.

4. Prepare handouts to support the programme. For example, one handout might restate critical points in the video while another provides a series of questions.

5. Make sure that you know how to use the video equipment and that it works as it should. Check the connections and controls are adjusted properly. Rehearse so that you can present the programme and the accompanying activities smoothly.

Using video

When you use video in your training session or presentation you might follow this sequence.

1. Prevent potential interruptions by disconnecting any phones and closing the door to the room.

2. Introduce the video and tell employees what they might pay attention to.

3. Tell them about the discussion or activities that follow the video. This will help employees focus on what they might learn from the programme. You might also challenge them with a question to be answered at the end of the video. This should be a question that is relevant to the objectives and personally interesting – one which obliges employees to apply the information from the video to their own personal or job situation. Alternatively, you might give employees a question sheet covering important information they should look for in the programme.

4. Darken the room enough for the video to be seen clearly, but leave some lights on so that employees can make notes.

5. Stay in the room while the video is on and model the attentive behaviour you expect of employees. Don't let them think the video is being shown just for you to have a break. Observe employees' reactions to the programme – this will help you decide how to approach the follow-up session.

6. Stop the video at intervals to discuss major steps in a particular process, the meaning of concepts or specific situations. These stop-go techniques engage employees' attention, prevent them getting overloaded with information and transform a one-way communication experience into an active one. But don't stop the programme for too long or too often. You might destroy the continuity of the programme or detract from the interest and

value of the follow-up activity. You might also find yourself short of time.

7. After the video you might:

- Repeat the question(s) you asked before the programme. These could lead into the follow-up task or discussion.
- Ask employees to work individually or in pairs to complete a questionnaire.
- Ask employees to work on an application task. This may involve them dividing into groups and finding ways to apply the video information to their own situations.
- Lead a discussion. First you might reinforce or elicit some of the key points made in the video, then ask how employees' experience relates to the programme and situations illustrated. Through the discussion you can integrate the purpose and content of the video with the rest of the training session.

References and Resources

General references and resources

R. Bennett (1989) *Effective Supervisory Management Series*, Volume 1: *Managing People*; Volume 2: *Managing Activities and Resources*; Volume 3: *Personal Effectiveness*, Kogan Page, London.

K. Blanchard and P. Hersey (1982 onwards) *Situational Leadership* series, Pfeiffer and Co. University Associates, San Diego, California.

K. Blanchard and S. Johnson (1983 onwards) *The One-Minute Manager* series, Fontana, London.

C. Handy (1989) *The Age of Unreason*, Business Books, London.

D. McGregor (1960) *The Human Side of Enterprise*, McGraw Hill, New York. (It's surprising how much managers and organizations can still learn from this classic text.)

T. Peters and N. Austin (1989) *A Passion for Excellence*, Random House, New York.

Training magazine published monthly by Lakewood Publications, Lakewood Building, 50 S. Ninth St, Minneapolis, MN 55402, USA.

Training and Development Journal published monthly by the American Society for Training and Development, 1640 King Street, Box 1443, Alexandria, VA 22313-2043, USA.

Training and Development published monthly by the British Institute of Training and Development, Marlow House, Institute Road, Marlow, Buckinghamshire SL7 1BN, England.

Videos from Video Arts Ltd, Dumbarton House, 68 Oxford Street, London W1N 9LA. Videos which can help you with specific skills are listed under the appropriate chapter heading.

Individual chapter references and resources

Chapter 1. Staff Development – Your Role in Improving Performance

J. Naisbitt and P. Aburdene (1990) *Megatrends 2000*, Pan Books, London. (A good source of statistics although you may disagree with some of the opinions expressed.)

Workforce 2000: Work and Workers for the 21st Century. (A 1987 demographic study commissioned by the US Department of Labor and conducted by the Hudson Institute of Indianapolis.)

European Community Labour Market Survey 1991. (This includes the statistics on skilled and unskilled labour quoted in Chapter 1.)

Chapter 2. How to Introduce New Staff to your Department

A. Fowler (1990) *A Good Start*, British Institute of Personnel Management.

M. Meighan (1991) *How to Design and Deliver Induction Training Programmes*, Kogan Page, London.

G.F. Shea (1981) *The New Employee*, Addison-Wesley Publishing, Reading, Massachusetts. (Information on induction programmes in the US.)

Chapter 3. How to Provide Mentoring and On-the-job Training

M. Murray (1991) *Beyond the Myths and Magic of Mentoring*, Jossey-Bass, San Francisco. (This book provides detailed information on setting up a systematic mentoring programme with lots of examples from US organizations.)

R. Buckley and J. Caple (1991) *One-to-One Training and Coaching Skills*, Kogan Page, London.

Video Arts Ltd: *You'll Soon Get The Hang Of It*. (This entertaining but very practical video shows managers, supervisors and foremen how to prepare for and conduct on-the-job training.)

Chapter 4. How to Prepare for a Group Training Session

D. Leigh (1991) *A Practical Approach to Group Training*, Kogan Page, London.

Chapter 5. How to Conduct a Group Training Session

D. Leigh (1991) *A Practical Approach to Group Training*, Kogan Page, London.

Chapter 6. How to Improve Performance through Off-the-job Training

D. McGregor (1960) *The Human Side of Enterprise*, McGraw Hill, New York.

The annual *Training Directory* published by Kogan Page gives information on consultants, course providers, training centres and equipment. You can easily locate suppliers of various training services. The *Directory* also provides information on the latest UK government training initiatives and the Training and Enterprise councils.

Chapter 7. How to Conduct Effective Team Meetings

M.E. Haynes (1988) *Effective Meeting Skills*, Kogan Page, London.

W. Fletcher (1984) *Meetings, Meetings*, William Morrow, New York. (An entertaining book on meeting strategy and the Machiavellian 'games' that meeting leaders and participants play.)

Video Arts Ltd: *Meetings, Bloody Meetings* and *More Bloody Meetings*. (These videos feature John Cleese as the manager running like a headless chicken from one meeting to another.)

Chapter 8. How to Delegate Work and Responsibilities

B. Maddux (1991) *Delegating for Results*, Kogan Page, London.

Chapter 9. How to Coach your People

T. Peters and N. Austin (1989) *A Passion for Excellence*, Warner Books, New York.

Video Arts Ltd: *Have you Got a Minute?* (A practical approach to coaching people at work with some clear do's and don'ts.)

Chapter 10. How to Conduct Effective Performance Reviews

R.B. Maddux (1988) *Effective Performance Appraisals*, Kogan Page, London.

Index

Index